Audio Access Included

TRUMPET
BY KEVIN JOHNSON
AEROBICS

Contents

To access audio visit:
www.halleonard.com/mylibrary
Enter Code
2930-4457-2073-8142

Cover Illustration by Birck Cox

ISBN 978-1-4803-9466-7

HAL•LEONARD®
CORPORATION
7777 W. BLUEMOUND RD. P.O. BOX 13819 MILWAUKEE, WI 53213

In Australia Contact:
Hal Leonard Australia Pty. Ltd.
4 Lentara Court
Cheltenham, Victoria, 3192 Australia
Email: ausadmin@halleonard.com.au

T0057663

Visit Hal Leonard Online at
www.halleonard.com

INTRODUCTION

When I was asked to write *Trumpet Aerobics*, I immediately thought of the vast assortment of excellent trumpet literature already available. How could I contribute to this world of trumpet instruction that has already been taught so thoroughly? I decided that the first part of my answer was in a new, simpler approach: a year-long systematic daily workout program that gradually increases in difficulty until all the techniques are mastered. The second part of my answer stemmed from my belief in the importance of being a well-rounded musician, which I addressed by introducing concepts of jazz and commercial playing and music theory. Concepts like these are essential for the modern trumpet player.

Only one exercise a day! How simple and, potentially, underwhelming. With only a few measures to practice each day, you might be tempted to play the exercise through once and call it a day. Don't do that! Never settle for less! Challenge yourself to play the exercise a number of times, each time trying to play more beautifully than the last.

I have broken down the entirety of trumpet technique into seven categories, one for each day of the week: scales, articulations, flexibility, intervals, finger technique, a hodge-podge category (buzzing, lip bends, low and high registers, soft attacks, ornaments, and extended technique), and etudes.

Mondays focus on scales, each increasing in difficulty based on the key signature. The majority of the 52 weeks is comprised of the major and minor scales in every key. After that, different modes are introduced. These modes are given in only one key, but I highly recommend transposing these exercises to learn them in all 12 keys.

Tuesday's articulation studies alternate between staccato, legato, accented, marcato, and staccatissimo passages, then combine these articulations together. Clarity is always the goal. By the end of the 52 weeks, I provide a few examples of jazz-style articulations.

Wednesdays are all about flexibility. The studies consist of 52 straight weeks of gradually intensifying lip slurs. The goal is to gradually coordinate your muscles to the point of complete ease.

The interval studies on **Thursdays** are comprised of three subsections that cycle over the course of the year. First are patterns, in which a set interval, for example, a major 3rd, ascends and descends the range of the trumpet. Second are arpeggios, in which the scale from Monday is arpeggiated. And third is expanding, in which the intervals gradually increase in range.

On **Fridays**, the finger studies challenge the right hand's dexterity and timing. There are a few different types of exercises in this category: agility, third finger, chromatic scales, and chromatic sequences.

Saturday's exercises contain a number of different techniques: buzzing, soft attacks, flow studies, upper and lower register playing, lip bends, pedal notes, ornaments, and effects/extended techniques.

Sundays allow you to stretch out. Every week you'll have a chance to play a short melody that incorporates the different elements practiced earlier in the week. Play music, not notes on a page! Use the audio tracks as a guide. Steal ideas you like, discard those you don't, and be sure to create your own.

A note about dynamics: Most of the exercises are written without a specific dynamic marking. Practice these exercises at all dynamics. Challenge yourself to create different characters through the music. Remember the reason we practice: to be able to play music. When you are in control of the trumpet, you are truly free to make art.

THE WARM-UP
Always start the day with a gentle warm-up. Everyone has a different way of doing this, so try things out and see what works best for you. Personally, I start with long tones and flow studies similar to the ones included in this book, but like I said, experiment with different routines until you have something you like.

POSTURE
Sit up straight, but always be comfortable. Any tension can sneak into your playing. Be able to take a full, relaxed breath every time.

ABOUT THE ONLINE AUDIO
On the title page of this book you will find a code that allows you to access the online demo tracks. You can listen to these online or download them. A demo track is available for each of the exercises. These are named numerically, according to the workout number. For example, Wednesday of Week 3 is Workout #17.

RECOMMENDED LISTENING

The importance of listening to music cannot be stressed enough! It is one of the most efficient and enjoyable ways to develop your ears and musicianship. In this day and age, we have at our fingertips the technology to hear the world's greatest musicians. Find your favorite players and constantly strive to reach their level of artistry. Live with these sounds and let them become a part of you. And at the very least, listen and be genuinely excited about the art of creating music.

SOLO

Alison Balsom	*Caprice*
Allen Vizzutti	*Carnival of Venus*
Hakan Hardenberger	*The Art of the Trumpet*
Jack Sutte	*Fanfare Alone*
James Ackley	*New American Works for Trumpet*
Maurice André	*Maurice André*
Michael Sachs	*Live From Severance Hall*
Phil Smith	*New York Legends; Contest Solos; Orchestral Excerpts for Trumpet*
Rafael Mendez	*The Legacy*
Ray Mase	*Trumpet in Our Time*
Robert Sullivan	*Treasures for Trumpet*
Ryan Anthony	*Ryan Anthony with Gary Beard*
Sergei Nakariakov	*From Moscow with Love*
Thomas Hooten	*Trumpet Call*
Tine Thing Helseth	*Tine; Storyteller*
Wynton Marsalis	*Carnival (with Eastman Wind Ensemble)*

ENSEMBLE

American Brass Quintet	*Jewels*
Black Dyke Band	*Symphonic Brass*
Blast!	*Blast!*
Center City Brass	*Street Song; Arnold, Ewald, Bozza, Maurer, Dahl & Calvert*
Empire Brass	*Firedance*
German Brass	*Wagner: Celebrating Wagner*
Mnozil Brass	everything on YouTube
Philadelphia Brass Ensemble, Cleveland Brass Ensemble, Chicago Brass Ensemble	
	The Antiphonal Music of Gabrieli
Canadian Brass	*Canadian Brass Takes Flight*
The New York Trumpet Ensemble	
	A Festival of Trumpets
Youngblood Brass Band	
	Center:Level:Roar

ORCHESTRAL

Bernstein	*West Side Story Suite, Overture to Candide*
Bruckner	*Symphony No. 4, Symphony No. 7*
Holst	*The Planets*
Mahler	*Symphony No. 1; Symphony No. 2; Symphony No. 5*
Strauss	*An Alpine Symphony, Ein Heldenleben, Also Sprach Zarathustra, Don Juan*
Mussorgsky/Ravel	*Pictures at an Exhibition*
Respighi	*Pines of Rome, Fountains of Rome*
Shostakovich	*Symphony No. 5, Festive Overture*
Stravinsky	*The Rite of Spring, Firebird Suite, Petrushka*
Tchaikovsky	*Symphony No. 4, Symphony No. 5, Symphony No. 6*

Listen to the New York Philharmonic Orchestra, Cleveland Orchestra, Chicago Symphony Orchestra, London Symphony Orchestra, or Berlin Philharmonic Orchestra play the brass-heavy works listed above.

JAZZ (SMALL GROUP)

Louis Armstrong	*Jazz Moods – Hot; In Person*
Clifford Brown	*The Definitive Clifford Brown*
Clark Terry	*Oscar Peterson Trio + One: Clark Terry*
Miles Davis	*Kind of Blue*
Lee Morgan	*Blue Train* (John Coltrane)
Freddie Hubbard	*Red Clay*
Maynard Ferguson	*This is Jazz #16*
Wynton Marsalis	*Standard Time; Keystone 3* (Art Blakey)
Roy Hargrove	*Distractions* (The RH Factor)
Ambrose Akinmusire	*When the Heart Emerges Glistening*

JAZZ (BIG BAND)

Count Basie Orchestra	*The Complete Atomic Basie; Frank Sinatra: The Best of the Capitol Years; Fun Time*
Duke Ellington Orchestra	
	Ellington '55; The Far East Suite
Stan Kenton	*Kenton's West Side Story; Cuban Fire!*
Thad Jones/Mel Lewis Orchestra	
	Consummation
The Vanguard Jazz Orchestra	
	Thad Jones Legacy
Lincoln Center Jazz Orchestra	
	Live in Swing City

ROCK/FUNK

Blood, Sweat & Tears	*Blood, Sweat & Tears; Greatest Hits*
Chicago	*Chicago Transit Authority; The Very Best Of: Only the Beginning* (disc 1)
Earth Wind and Fire	*That's the Way of the World; Greatest Hits*
Reel Big Fish	*Turn the Radio Off*
Snarky Puppy	*groundUP; We Like It Here*
Streetlight Manifesto	*Everything Goes Numb*
Tower of Power	*Tower of Power; Soul Vaccination: Tower of Power Live*

FINGERING CHART
(WITH ALTERNATE FINGERINGS)

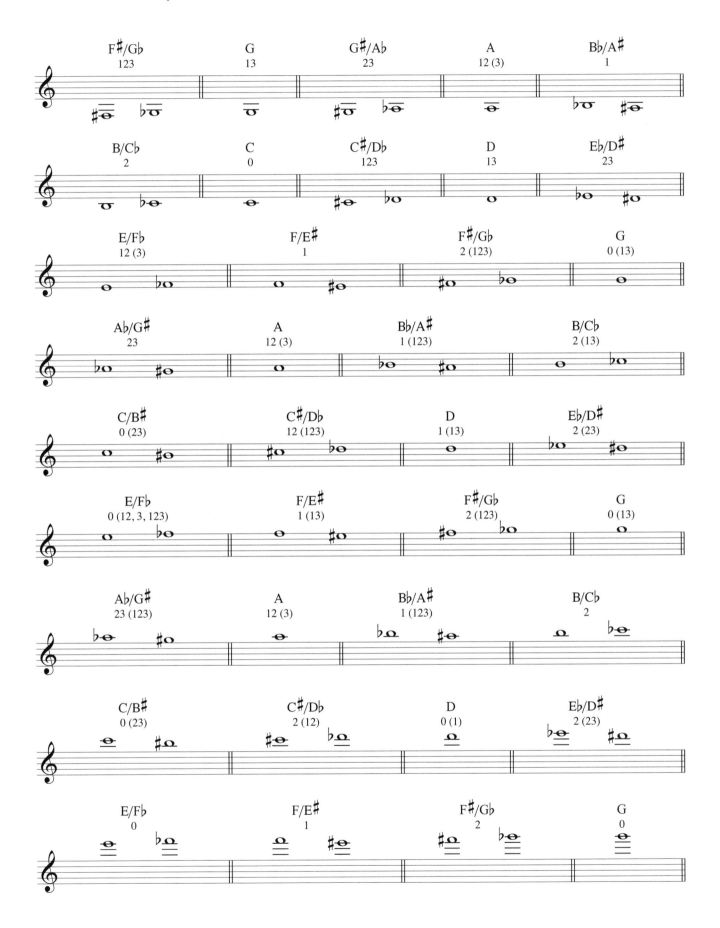

MON

Workout #1   **Type:** Scale   **Sub-type:** C major
Goals: 1) To develop an even, beautiful sound across the full range of the trumpet; 2) To reach the point in which you are no longer consciously thinking about the fingerings.
Tip: Start slowly and gradually increase the speed. Repeat the exercise a number of times until the fingerings become natural and subconscious.

TUE

Workout #2   **Type:** Articulation   **Sub-type:** Legato
Goal: To produce a pure tone that fluidly connects to the next note without a break.
Tip: Practice by imagining you are playing one single long tone, barely nicking the air to initiate each new note.

WED

Workout #3   **Type:** Flexibility
Goal: To play relaxed, uninterrupted transitions between the partials of the trumpet.
Tip: Focus on the fact that you are simply playing one long steady stream of air. Imagining the sounds "tah" on lower notes and "ee" on upper notes may help move your air.

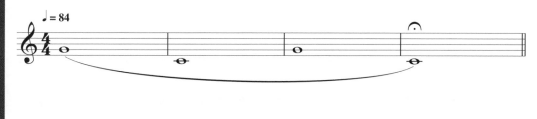

THU

Workout #4　　　**Type:** Interval　　　**Sub-type:** Pattern

Goal: To hear each interval in your head, and then to execute it through the trumpet.

Tip: Try singing these exercises to ensure that your ears are truly hearing each note.

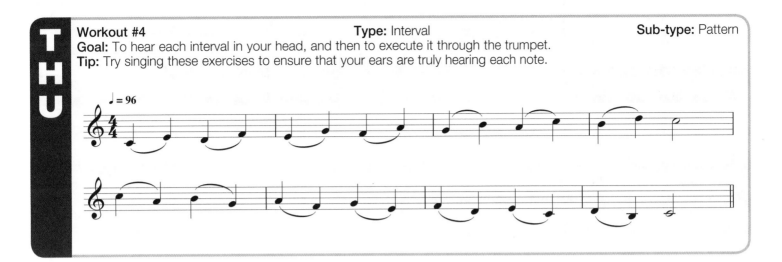

FRI

Workout #5　　　**Type:** Fingers　　　**Sub-type:** Agility

Goal: To achieve agile, in-time, dexterous fingers.

Tip: Use a metronome and subdivide in your head. Every note should be perfectly in time.

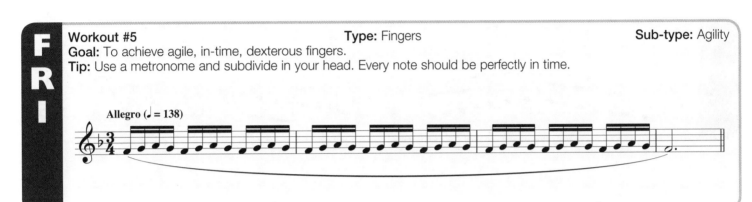

SAT

Workout #6　　　**Type:** Variety　　　**Sub-type:** Buzzing

Goal: To produce a pure and vibrant-sounding buzz.

Tip: Before making a sound, make sure you have the correct starting pitch by first either playing it on the trumpet or another instrument (like a piano).

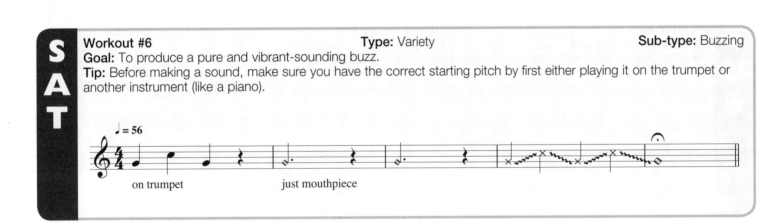

SUN

Workout #7　　　**Type:** Etude　　　**Sub-type:** C major

Goal: To play musically and beautifully by utilizing the skills developed over the course of the week.

Tip: Use the written dynamics to help shape your phrasing.

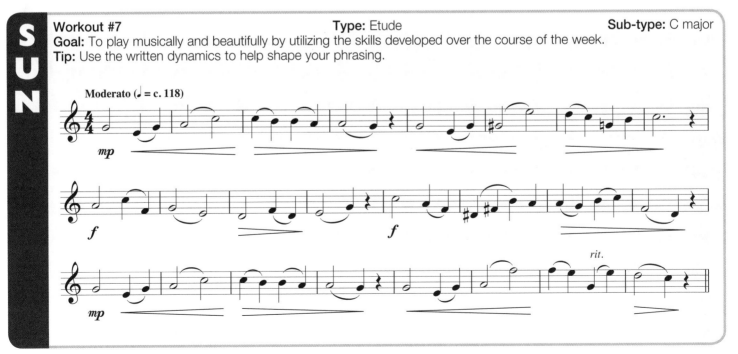

MON

Workout #8   **Type:** Scale   **Sub-type:** F major

Goals: 1) To develop an even, beautiful sound across the full range of the trumpet; 2) To reach the point in which you are no longer consciously thinking about the fingerings.

Tip: Start slowly and gradually increase the speed. Repeat the exercise a number of times until the fingerings become natural and subconscious.

TUE

Workout #9   **Type:** Articulation   **Sub-type:** Staccato

Goal: To produce a full-bodied tone that is detached from the other notes.

Tip: Do not stop each note with your tongue. Let your air create the desired note length.

WED

Workout #10   **Type:** Flexibility

Goal: To play relaxed, uninterrupted transitions between the partials of the trumpet.

Tip: Focus on the fact that you are simply playing one long steady stream of air. Imagining the sounds "tah" on lower notes and "ee" on upper notes may help move your air.

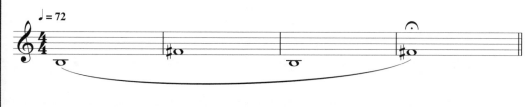

Workout #11 **Type:** Interval **Sub-type:** Arpeggio

Goal: To hear each interval in your head, and then to execute it through the trumpet.

Tip: Try singing these exercises to ensure that your ears are truly hearing each note.

Workout #12 **Type:** Fingers **Sub-type:** Agility

Goal: To achieve agile, in-time, dexterous fingers.

Tip: Use a metronome and subdivide in your head. Every note should be perfectly in time.

Workout #13 **Type:** Variety **Sub-type:** Buzzing

Goal: To produce a pure and vibrant-sounding buzz.

Tip: Before making a sound, make sure you have the correct starting pitch by first either playing it on the trumpet or another instrument (like a piano).

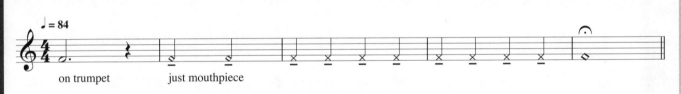

on trumpet   just mouthpiece

Workout #14 **Type:** Etude **Sub-type:** F major

Goal: To play musically and beautifully by utilizing the skills developed over the course of the week.

WEEK 3

MON

Workout #15   **Type:** Scale   **Sub-type:** G major
Goals: 1) To develop an even, beautiful sound across the full range of the trumpet; 2) To reach the point in which you are no longer consciously thinking about the fingerings.
Tip: Start slowly and gradually increase the speed. Repeat the exercise a number of times until the fingerings become natural and subconscious.

TUE

Workout #16   **Type:** Articulation   **Sub-type:** Accent
Goal: To produce a strong, front-heavy articulation that is followed by a sustained and energized sound.
Tip: Keep the air moving in order to keep the sound activated throughout the entire duration of the note.

WED

Workout #17   **Type:** Flexibility
Goal: To play relaxed, uninterrupted transitions between the partials of the trumpet.
Tip: Focus on the fact that you are simply playing one long steady stream of air. Imagining the sounds "tah" on lower notes and "ee" on upper notes may help move your air.

THU

Workout #18   **Type:** Interval   **Sub-type:** Expanding

Goal: To hear each interval in your head, and then to execute it through the trumpet.

Tip: Try singing these exercises to ensure that your ears are truly hearing each note. Imagine the wider intervals as being close together and easy to execute.

FRI

Workout #19   **Type:** Fingers   **Sub-type:** Agility

Goal: To achieve agile, in-time, dexterous fingers.

Tip: Use a metronome and subdivide in your head. Every note should be perfectly in time.

SAT

Workout #20   **Type:** Variety   **Sub-type:** Buzzing

Goal: To produce a pure and vibrant-sounding buzz.

Tip: Before making a sound, make sure you have the correct starting pitch by first either playing it on the trumpet or another instrument (like a piano).

SUN

Workout #21   **Type:** Etude   **Sub-type:** G major

Goal: To play musically and beautifully by utilizing the skills developed over the course of the week.

MON

Workout #22 **Type:** Scale **Sub-type:** B♭ major
Goals: 1) To develop an even, beautiful sound across the full range of the trumpet; 2) To reach the point in which you are no longer consciously thinking about the fingerings.
Tip: Start slowly and gradually increase the speed. Repeat the exercise a number of times until the fingerings become natural and subconscious.

TUE

Workout #23 **Type:** Articulation **Sub-type:** Legato
Goal: To produce a pure tone that fluidly connects to the next note without a break.
Tip: Practice by imagining you are playing one single long tone, barely nicking the air to initiate each new note.

WED

Workout #24 **Type:** Flexibility
Goal: To play relaxed, uninterrupted transitions between the partials of the trumpet.
Tip: Focus on the fact that you are simply playing one long steady stream of air. Imagining the sounds "tah" on lower notes and "ee" on upper notes may help move your air.

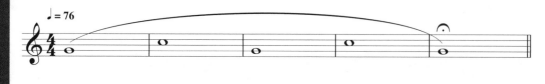

THU

Workout #25 **Type:** Interval **Sub-type:** Pattern

Goal: To hear each interval in your head, and then to execute it through the trumpet.
Tip: Try singing these exercises to ensure that your ears are truly hearing each note.

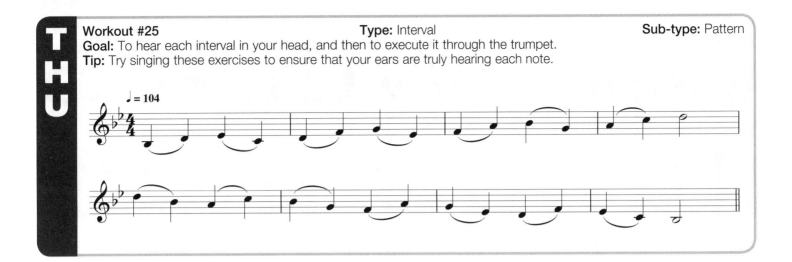

FRI

Workout #26 **Type:** Fingers **Sub-type:** Agility

Goal: To achieve agile, in-time, dexterous fingers.
Tip: Use a metronome and subdivide in your head. Every note should be perfectly in time.

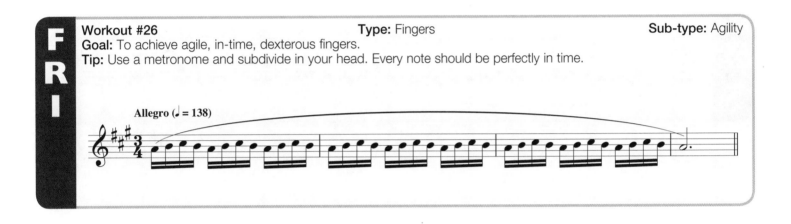

SAT

Workout #27 **Type:** Variety **Sub-type:** Low register

Goal: To produce full and relaxed low notes.
Tip: Use plenty of warm air, the same kind of air you would use to fog a pane of glass.

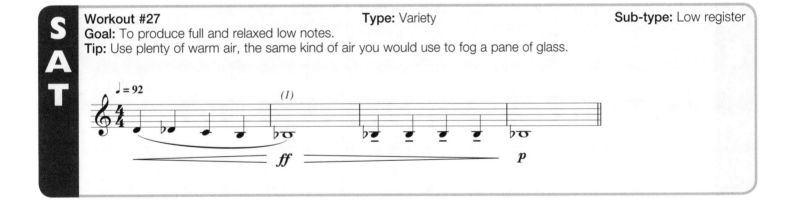

SUN

Workout #28 **Type:** Etude **Sub-type:** B♭ major

Goal: To play musically and beautifully by utilizing the skills developed over the course of the week.

MON

Workout #29   **Type:** Scale   **Sub-type:** D major

Goals: 1) To develop an even, beautiful sound across the full range of the trumpet; 2) To reach the point in which you are no longer consciously thinking about the fingerings.

Tip: Start slowly and gradually increase the speed. Repeat the exercise a number of times until the fingerings become natural and subconscious.

TUE

Workout #30   **Type:** Articulation   **Sub-type:** Staccato

Goal: To produce a full-bodied tone that is detached from the other notes.

Tip: Do not stop each note with your tongue. Let your air create the desired note length.

WED

Workout #31   **Type:** Flexibility

Goal: To play relaxed, uninterrupted transitions between the partials of the trumpet.

Tip: Focus on the fact that you are simply playing one long steady stream of air. Imagining the sounds "tah" on lower notes and "ee" on upper notes may help move your air.

THU

Workout #32 **Type:** Interval **Sub-type:** Arpeggio

Goal: To hear each interval in your head, and then to execute it through the trumpet.

Tip: Try singing these exercises to ensure that your ears are truly hearing each note.

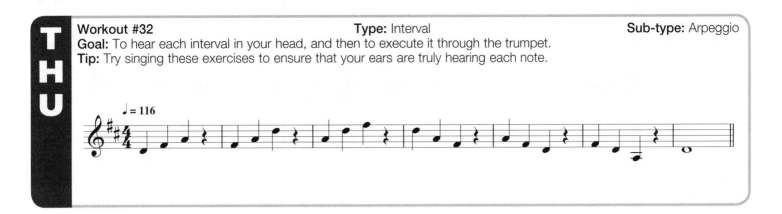

FRI

Workout #33 **Type:** Fingers **Sub-type:** Agility

Goal: To achieve agile, in-time, dexterous fingers.

Tip: Use a metronome and subdivide in your head. Every note should be perfectly in time.

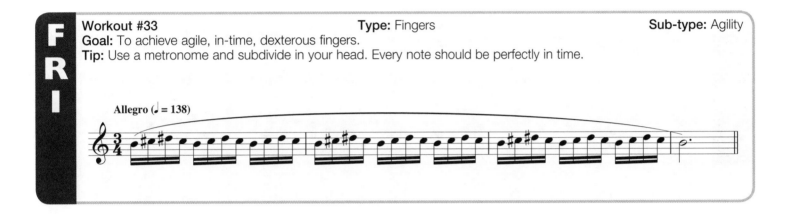

SAT

Workout #34 **Type:** Variety **Sub-type:** Low register

Goal: To produce full and relaxed low notes.

Tip: Use plenty of warm air, the same kind of air you would use to fog a pane of glass.

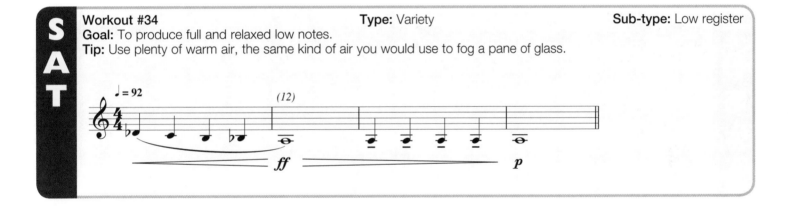

SUN

Workout #35 **Type:** Etude **Sub-type:** D major

Goal: To play musically and beautifully by utilizing the skills developed over the course of the week.

Tip: Don't play this etude too choppy or disjunct. Always blow through the musical line.

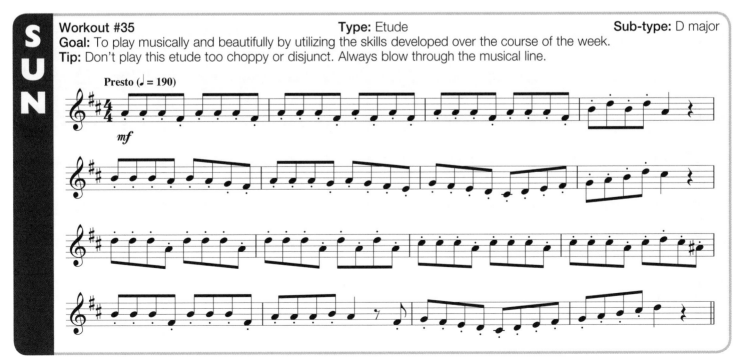

MON

Workout #36 **Type:** Scale **Sub-type:** Eb major
Goals: 1) To develop an even, beautiful sound across the full range of the trumpet; 2) To reach the point in which you are no longer consciously thinking about the fingerings.
Tip: Start slowly and gradually increase the speed. Repeat the exercise a number of times until the fingerings become natural and subconscious.

TUE

Workout #37 **Type:** Articulation **Sub-type:** Legato
Goal: To produce a pure tone that fluidly connects to the next note without a break.
Tip: Practice by imagining you are playing one single long tone, barely nicking the air to initiate each new note.

WED

Workout #38 **Type:** Flexibility
Goal: To play relaxed, uninterrupted transitions between the partials of the trumpet.
Tip: Focus on the fact that you are simply playing one long steady stream of air. Imagining the sounds "tah" on lower notes and "ee" on upper notes may help move your air.

THU

Workout #39 **Type:** Interval **Sub-type:** Expanding

Goal: To hear each interval in your head, and then to execute it through the trumpet.

Tip: Try singing these exercises to ensure that your ears are truly hearing each note. Imagine the wider intervals as being close together and easy to execute.

FRI

Workout #40 **Type:** Fingers **Sub-type:** Chromatic half-octave

Goal: To achieve agile, in-time, dexterous fingers.

Tip: Use a metronome and subdivide in your head. Every note should be perfectly in time.

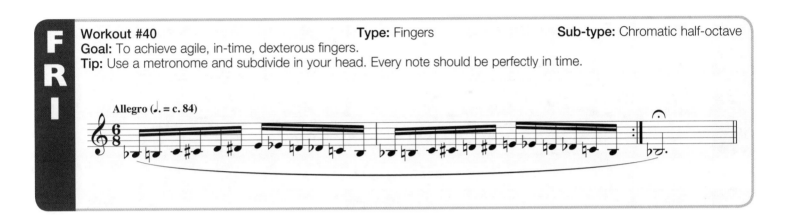

SAT

Workout #41 **Type:** Variety **Sub-type:** Low register

Goal: To produce full and relaxed low notes.

Tip: Use plenty of warm air, the same kind of air you would use to fog a pane of glass.

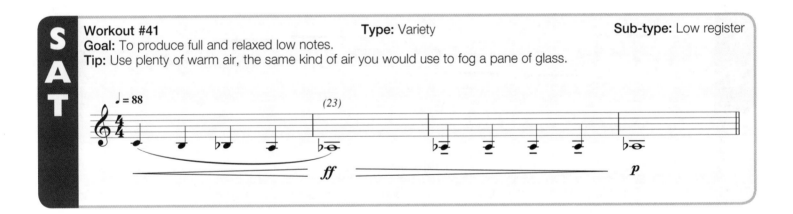

SUN

Workout #42 **Type:** Etude **Sub-type:** E♭ major

Goal: To play musically and beautifully by utilizing the skills developed over the course of the week.

MON

Workout #43 **Type:** Scale **Sub-type:** A major

Goals: 1) To develop an even, beautiful sound across the full range of the trumpet; 2) To reach the point in which you are no longer consciously thinking about the fingerings.

Tip: Start slowly and gradually increase the speed. Repeat the exercise a number of times until the fingerings become natural and subconscious.

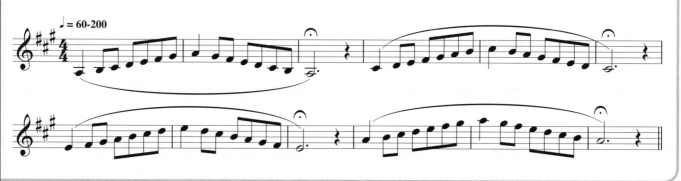

TUE

Workout #44 **Type:** Articulation **Sub-type:** Staccato

Goal: To produce a full-bodied tone that is detached from the other notes.

Tip: Do not stop each note with your tongue. Let your air create the desired note length.

WED

Workout #45 **Type:** Flexibility

Goal: To play relaxed, uninterrupted transitions between the partials of the trumpet.

Tip: Focus on the fact that you are simply playing one long steady stream of air. Imagining the sounds "tah" on lower notes and "ee" on upper notes may help move your air.

THU

Workout #46 **Type:** Interval **Sub-type:** Pattern

Goal: To hear each interval in your head, and then to execute it through the trumpet.

Tip: Try singing these exercises to ensure that your ears are truly hearing each note.

Workout #47 **Type:** Fingers **Sub-type:** Chromatic half-octave

Goal: To achieve agile, in-time, dexterous fingers.

Tip: Use a metronome and subdivide in your head. Every note should be perfectly in time.

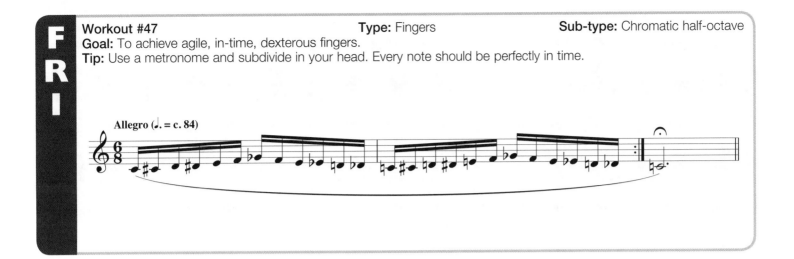

Workout #48 **Type:** Variety **Sub-type:** Low register

Goal: To produce full and relaxed low notes.

Tip: Use plenty of warm air, the same kind of air you would use to fog a pane of glass.

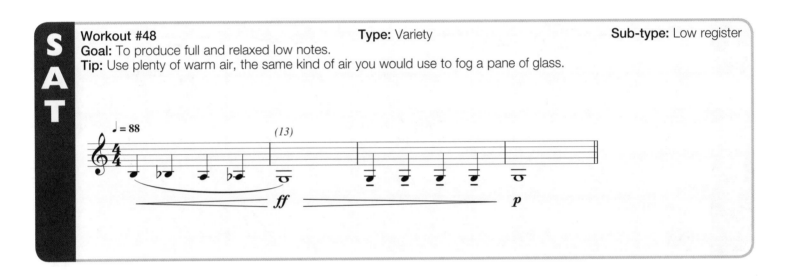

Workout #49 **Type:** Etude **Sub-type:** A major

Goal: To play musically and beautifully by utilizing the skills developed over the course of the week.

Tip: Create a completely new character in the middle *piano* section.

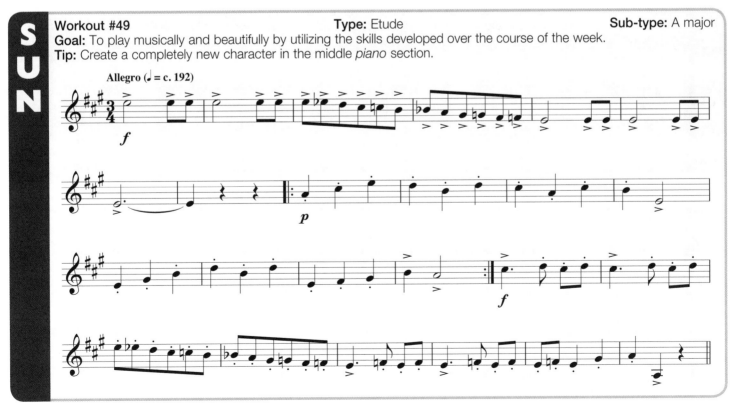

MON

Workout #50 **Type:** Scale **Sub-type:** A♭ major
Goals: 1) To develop an even, beautiful sound across the full range of the trumpet; 2) To reach the point in which you are no longer consciously thinking about the fingerings.
Tip: Start slowly and gradually increase the speed. Repeat the exercise a number of times until the fingerings become natural and subconscious.

TUE

Workout #51 **Type:** Articulation **Sub-type:** Accent
Goal: To produce a strong, front-heavy articulation that is followed by a sustained and energized sound.
Tip: Keep the air moving in order to keep the sound activated throughout the entire duration of the note.

WED

Workout #52 **Type:** Flexibility
Goal: To play relaxed, uninterrupted transitions between the partials of the trumpet.
Tip: Focus on the fact that you are simply playing one long steady stream of air. Imagining the sounds "tah" on lower notes and "ee" on upper notes may help move your air.

THU

Workout #53 **Type:** Interval **Sub-type:** Arpeggio
Goal: To hear each interval in your head, and then to execute it through the trumpet.
Tip: Try singing these exercises to ensure that your ears are truly hearing each note.

FRI

Workout #54   **Type:** Fingers   **Sub-type:** Chromatic half-octave

Goal: To achieve agile, in-time, dexterous fingers.

Tip: Use a metronome and subdivide in your head. Every note should be perfectly in time.

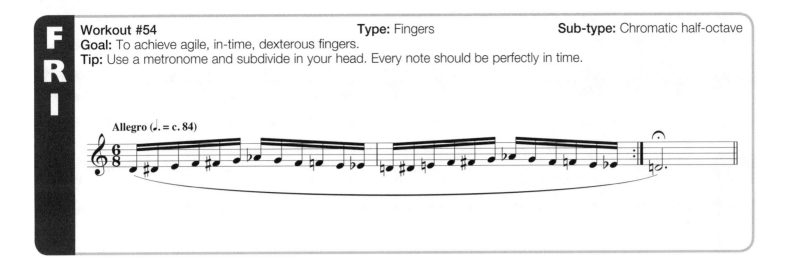

SAT

Workout #55   **Type:** Variety   **Sub-type:** Low register

Goal: To produce full and relaxed low notes.

Tip: Use plenty of warm air, the same kind of air you would use to fog a pane of glass.

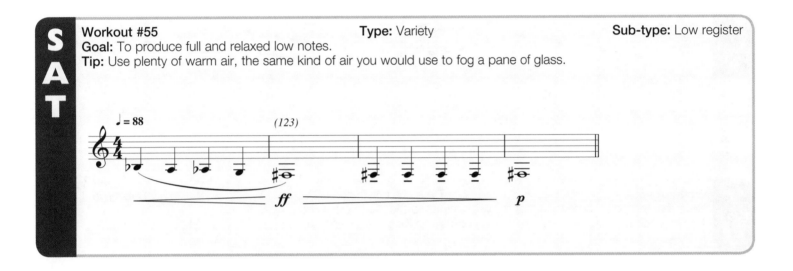

SUN

Workout #56   **Type:** Etude   **Sub-type:** A♭ major

Goal: To play musically and beautifully by utilizing the skills developed over the course of the week.

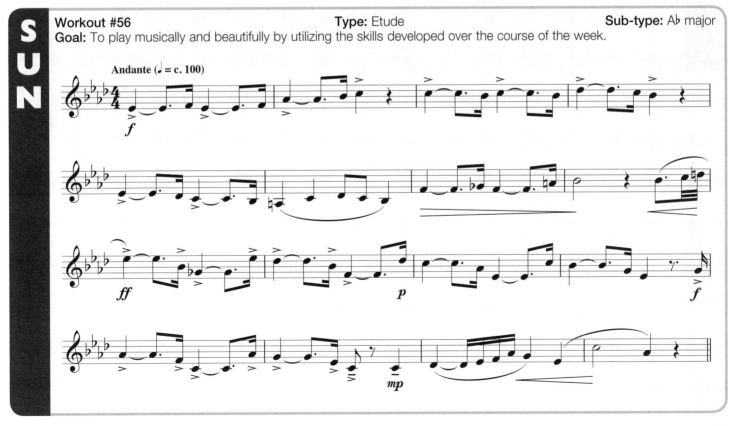

MON

Workout #57 **Type:** Scale **Sub-type:** E major
Goals: 1) To develop an even, beautiful sound across the full range of the trumpet; 2) To reach the point in which you are no longer consciously thinking about the fingerings.
Tip: Start slowly and gradually increase the speed. Repeat the exercise a number of times until the fingerings become natural and subconscious.

TUE

Workout #58 **Type:** Articulation **Sub-type:** Legato
Goal: To produce a pure tone that fluidly connects to the next note without a break.
Tip: Practice by imagining you are playing one single long tone, barely nicking the air to initiate each new note.

WED

Workout #59 **Type:** Flexibility
Goal: To play relaxed, uninterrupted transitions between the partials of the trumpet.
Tip: Focus on the fact that you are simply playing one long steady stream of air. Imagining the sounds "tah" on lower notes and "ee" on upper notes may help move your air.

THU

Workout #60

Type: Interval   **Sub-type:** Expanding

Goal: To hear each interval in your head, and then to execute it through the trumpet.
Tip: Try singing these exercises to ensure that your ears are truly hearing each note. Imagine the wider intervals as being close together and easy to execute.

FRI

Workout #61

Type: Fingers   **Sub-type:** Chromatic half-octave

Goal: To achieve agile, in-time, dexterous fingers.
Tip: Use a metronome and subdivide in your head. Every note should be perfectly in time.

SAT

Workout #62

Type: Variety   **Sub-type:** Soft attacks

Goal: To use a gentle attack that produces a quiet note without interruption.
Tip: Stay relaxed. Tension will keep the notes from speaking.

SUN

Workout #63

Type: Etude   **Sub-type:** E major

Goal: To play musically and beautifully by utilizing the skills developed over the course of the week.
Tip: Always decide where the musical climax should be and arc your phrasing accordingly. In this particular melody, the climax is located four measures from the end.

MON

Workout #64   **Type:** Scale   **Sub-type:** D♭ major
Goals: 1) To develop an even, beautiful sound across the full range of the trumpet; 2) To reach the point in which you are no longer consciously thinking about the fingerings.
Tip: Start slowly and gradually increase the speed. Repeat the exercise a number of times until the fingerings become natural and subconscious.

TUE

Workout #65   **Type:** Articulation   **Sub-type:** Accent
Goal: To produce a strong, front-heavy articulation that is followed by a sustained and energized sound.
Tip: Keep the air moving in order to keep the sound activated throughout the entire duration of the note.

WED

Workout #66   **Type:** Flexibility
Goal: To play relaxed, uninterrupted transitions between the partials of the trumpet.
Tip: Focus on the fact that you are simply playing one long steady stream of air. Imagining the sounds "tah" on lower notes and "ee" on upper notes may help move your air.

THU

Workout #67 **Type:** Interval **Sub-type:** Pattern

Goal: To hear each interval in your head, and then to execute it through the trumpet.

Tip: Try singing these exercises to ensure that your ears are truly hearing each note.

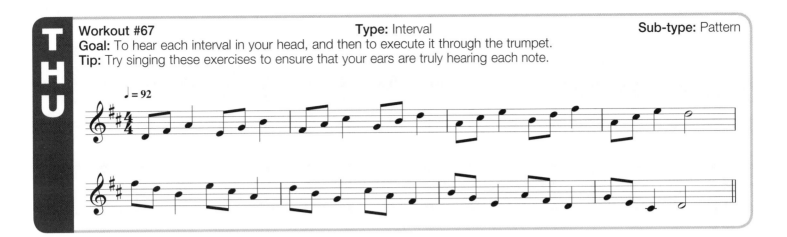

FRI

Workout #68 **Type:** Fingers **Sub-type:** Chromatic half-octave

Goal: To achieve agile, in-time, dexterous fingers.

Tip: Use a metronome and subdivide in your head. Every note should be perfectly in time.

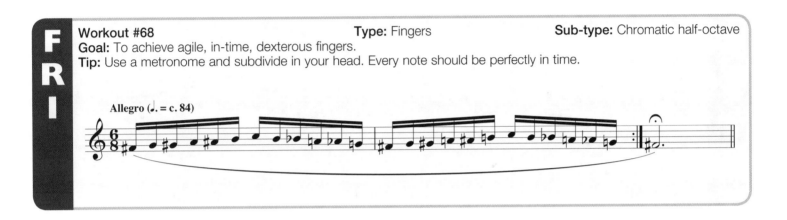

SAT

Workout #69 **Type:** Variety **Sub-type:** Soft attacks

Goal: To use a gentle attack that produces a quiet note without interruption.

Tip: Stay relaxed. Tension will keep the notes from speaking.

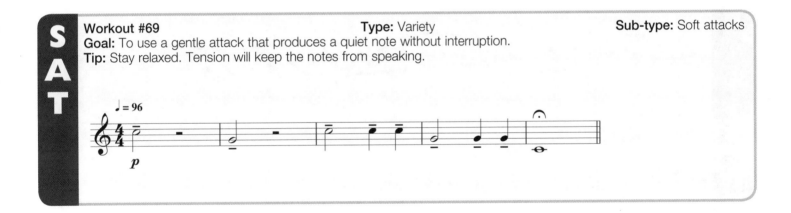

SUN

Workout #70 **Type:** Etude **Sub-type:** D♭ major

Goal: To play musically and beautifully by utilizing the skills developed over the course of the week.

Tip: Be deliberate with the three different types of articulations found in this etude.

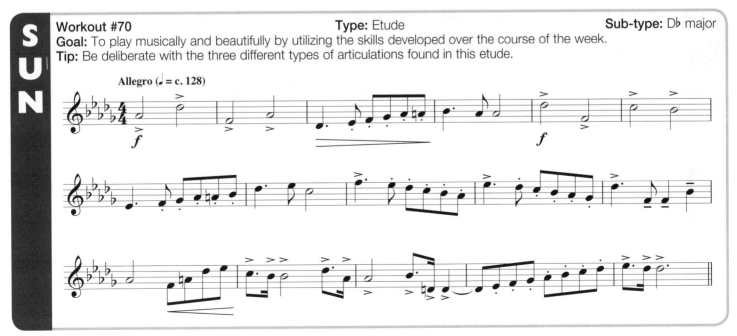

MON

Workout #71 **Type:** Scale **Sub-type:** B major
Goals: 1) To develop an even, beautiful sound across the full range of the trumpet; 2) To reach the point in which you are no longer consciously thinking about the fingerings.
Tip: Start slowly and gradually increase the speed. Repeat the exercise a number of times until the fingerings become natural and subconscious.

TUE

Workout #72 **Type:** Articulation **Sub-type:** Slur two, tongue two
Goal: To transition seamlessly between slurred notes and tongued notes.
Tip: Keep the second slurred note long and unclipped. This will keep your air moving.

WED

Workout #73 **Type:** Flexibility
Goal: To play relaxed, uninterrupted transitions between the partials of the trumpet.
Tip: Focus on the fact that you are simply playing one long steady stream of air. Imagining the sounds "tah" on lower notes and "ee" on upper notes may help move your air.

THU

Workout #74 **Type:** Interval **Sub-type:** Arpeggio
Goal: To hear each interval in your head, and then to execute it through the trumpet.
Tip: Try singing these exercises to ensure that your ears are truly hearing each note.

Workout #75 **Type:** Fingers **Sub-type:** Chromatic half-octave

Goal: To achieve agile, in-time, dexterous fingers

Tip: Use a metronome and subdivide in your head. Every note should be perfectly in time.

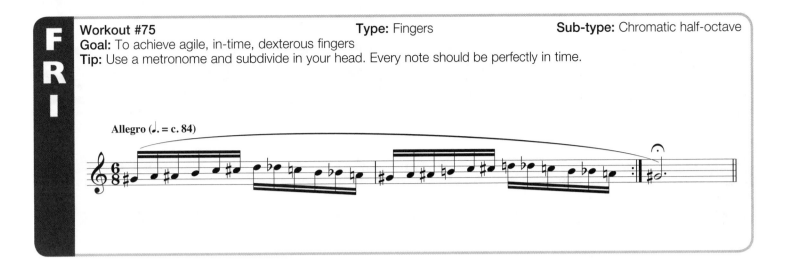

Workout #76 **Type:** Variety **Sub-type:** Soft attacks

Goal: To use a gentle attack that produces a quiet note without interruption.

Tip: Stay relaxed. Tension will keep the notes from speaking.

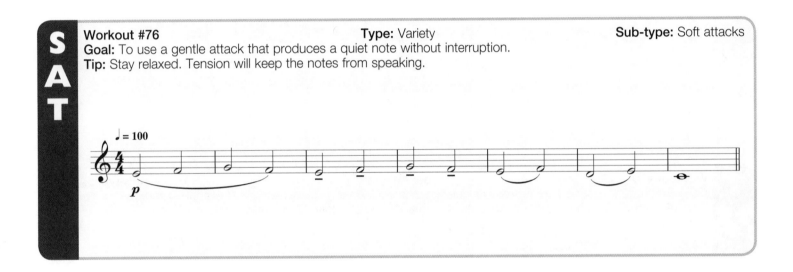

Workout #77 **Type:** Etude **Sub-type:** B major

Goal: To play musically and beautifully by utilizing the skills developed over the course of the week.

Tip: Play notably under tempo at first to work out the tricky chromaticism.

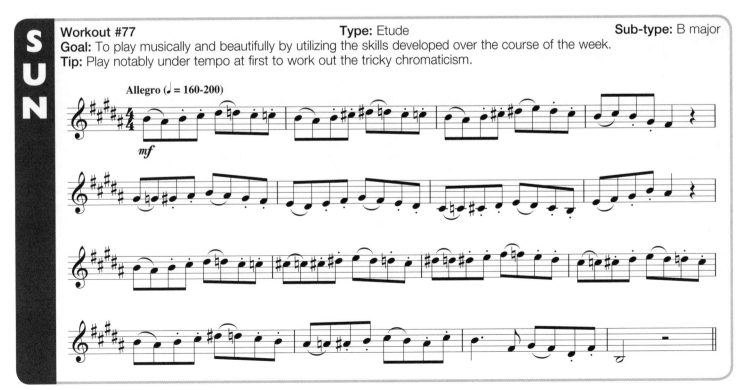

MON

Workout #78 **Type:** Scale **Sub-type:** F# major
Goals: 1) To develop an even, beautiful sound across the full range of the trumpet; 2) To reach the point in which you are no longer consciously thinking about the fingerings.
Tip: Start slowly and gradually increase the speed. Repeat the exercise a number of times until the fingerings become natural and subconscious.

TUE

Workout #79 **Type:** Articulation **Sub-type:** Accent
Goal: To produce a strong, front-heavy articulation that is followed by a sustained and energized sound.
Tip: Keep the air moving in order to keep the sound activated throughout the entire duration of the note.

WED

Workout #80 **Type:** Flexibility
Goal: To play relaxed, uninterrupted transitions between the partials of the trumpet.
Tip: Focus on the fact that you are simply playing one long steady stream of air. Imagining the sounds "tah" on lower notes and "ee" on upper notes may help move your air.

Workout #81 **Type:** Interval **Sub-type:** Expanding

Goal: To hear each interval in your head, and then to execute it through the trumpet.

Tip: Try singing these exercises to ensure that your ears are truly hearing each note. Imagine the wider intervals as being close together and easy to execute.

Workout #82 **Type:** Fingers **Sub-type:** Chromatic half-octave

Goal: To achieve agile, in-time, dexterous fingers.

Tip: Use a metronome and subdivide in your head. Every note should be perfectly in time.

Workout #83 **Type:** Variety **Sub-type:** Soft attacks

Goal: To use a gentle attack that produces a quiet note without interruption.

Tip: Stay relaxed. Tension will keep the notes from speaking.

Workout #84 **Type:** Etude **Sub-type:** F# major

Goal: To play musically and beautifully by utilizing the skills developed over the course of the week.

Tip: Play loud and strong, but never become harsh.

WEEK 13

MON

Workout #85   **Type:** Scale   **Sub-type:** A natural minor, A harmonic minor

Goals: 1) To develop an even, beautiful sound across the full range of the trumpet; 2) To reach the point in which you are no longer consciously thinking about the fingerings.

Tip: Start slowly and gradually increase the speed. Repeat the exercise a number of times until the fingerings become natural and subconscious.

natural minor   harmonic minor

TUE

Workout #86   **Type:** Articulation   **Sub-type:** Legato

Goal: To produce a pure tone that fluidly connects to the next note without a break.

Tip: Practice by imagining you are playing one single long tone, barely nicking the air to initiate each new note.

WED

Workout #87   **Type:** Flexibility

Goal: To play relaxed, uninterrupted transitions between the partials of the trumpet.

Tip: Focus on the fact that you are simply playing one long steady stream of air. Imagining the sounds "tah" on lower notes and "ee" on upper notes may help move your air.

Workout #88   **Type:** Interval   **Sub-type:** Pattern
Goal: To hear each interval in your head, and then to execute it through the trumpet.
Tip: Try singing these exercises to ensure that your ears are truly hearing each note.

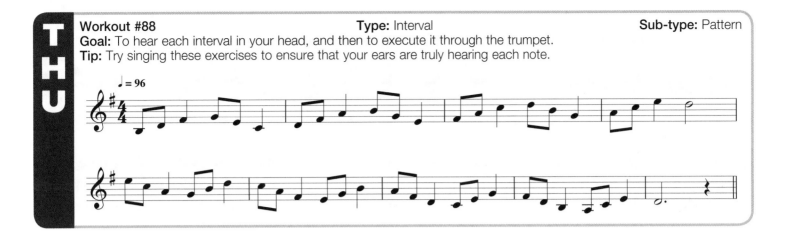

Workout #89   **Type:** Fingers   **Sub-type:** Chromatic half-octave
Goal: To achieve agile, in-time, dexterous fingers.
Tip: Use a metronome and subdivide in your head. Every note should be perfectly in time.

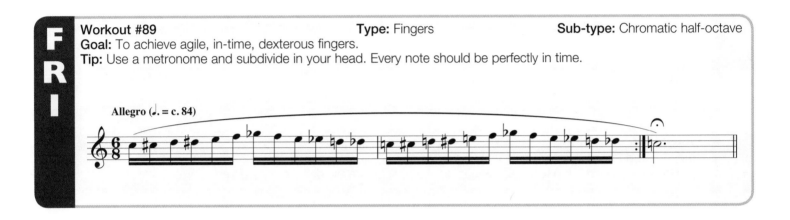

Workout #90   **Type:** Variety   **Sub-type:** Flow study
Goal: To produce an easy, connected, rich sound throughout the entire range of the trumpet.
Tip: Pretend that you are playing a single long tone with one long steady stream of air.

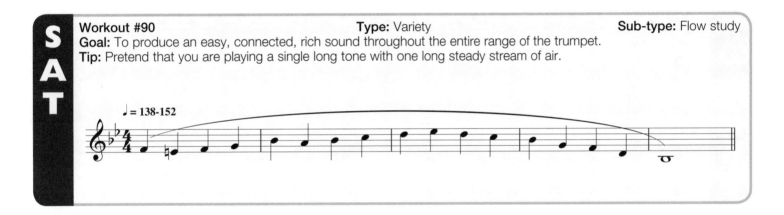

Workout #91   **Type:** Etude   **Sub-type:** A minor
Goal: To play musically and beautifully by utilizing the skills developed over the course of the week.
Tip: Experiment with stretching the time during the rubato measures.

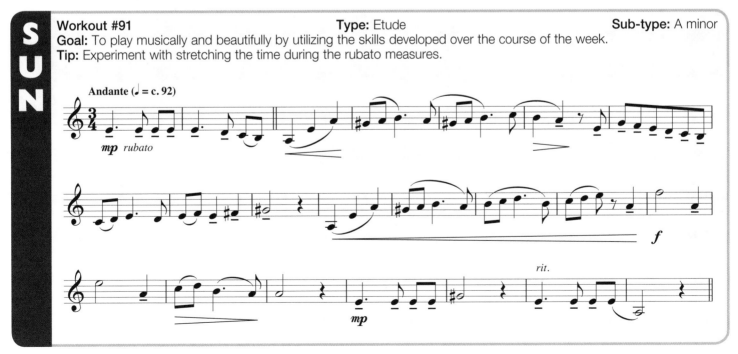

MON

Workout #92   Type: Scale   Sub-type: D natural minor, D harmonic minor
Goals: 1) To develop an even, beautiful sound across the full range of the trumpet; 2) To reach the point in which you are no longer consciously thinking about the fingerings.
Tip: Start slowly and gradually increase the speed. Repeat the exercise a number of times until the fingerings become natural and subconscious.

natural minor   harmonic minor

TUE

Workout #93   Type: Articulation   Sub-type: Staccato
Goal: To produce a full-bodied tone that is detached from the other notes.
Tip: Do not stop each note with your tongue. Let your air create the desired note length.

WED

Workout #94   Type: Flexibility
Goal: To play relaxed, uninterrupted transitions between the partials of the trumpet.
Tip: Focus on the fact that you are simply playing one long steady stream of air. Imagining the sounds "tah" on lower notes and "ee" on upper notes may help move your air.

THU

Workout #95   Type: Interval   Sub-type: Arpeggio
Goal: To hear each interval in your head, and then to execute it through the trumpet.
Tip: Try singing these exercises to ensure that your ears are truly hearing each note.

FRI

Workout #96   **Type:** Fingers   **Sub-type:** Third finger

Goal: To develop dexterity and control of the third finger.

Tip: Using the third finger feels awkward at first. Practice will promote the finger's independence.

SAT

Workout #97   **Type:** Variety   **Sub-type:** Flow study

Goal: To produce an easy, connected, rich sound throughout the entire range of the trumpet.

Tip: Pretend that you are playing a single long tone with one long steady stream of air.

SUN

Workout #98   **Type:** Etude   **Sub-type:** D minor "third valve"

Goal: To play musically and beautifully by utilizing the skills developed over the course of the week.

Tip: Practice slowly at first to ensure that your third finger doesn't fumble.

MON

Workout #99   **Type:** Scale   **Sub-type:** E natural minor, E harmonic minor
Goals: 1) To develop an even, beautiful sound across the full range of the trumpet; 2) To reach the point in which you are no longer consciously thinking about the fingerings.
Tip: Start slowly and gradually increase the speed. Repeat the exercise a number of times until the fingerings become natural and subconscious.

TUE

Workout #100   **Type:** Articulation   **Sub-type:** Legato
Goal: To produce a pure tone that fluidly connects to the next note without a break.
Tip: Practice by imagining you are playing one single long tone, barely nicking the air to initiate each new note.

WED

Workout #101   **Type:** Flexibility
Goal: To play relaxed, uninterrupted transitions between the partials of the trumpet.
Tip: Focus on the fact that you are simply playing one long steady stream of air. Imagining the sounds "tah" on lower notes and "ee" on upper notes may help move your air.

THU

Workout #102 **Type:** Interval **Sub-type:** Expanding

Goal: To hear each interval in your head, and then to execute it through the trumpet.

Tip: Try singing these exercises to ensure that your ears are truly hearing each note. Imagine the wider intervals as being close together and easy to execute.

FRI

Workout #103 **Type:** Fingers **Sub-type:** Third finger

Goal: To develop dexterity and control of the third finger.

Tip: Using the third finger feels awkward at first. Practice will promote the finger's independence.

SAT

Workout #104 **Type:** Variety **Sub-type:** Flow study

Goal: To produce an easy, connected, rich sound throughout the entire range of the trumpet.

Tip: Pretend that you are playing a single long tone with one long steady stream of air.

SUN

Workout #105 **Type:** Etude **Sub-type:** E minor

Goal: To play musically and beautifully by utilizing the skills developed over the course of the week.

Tip: Experiment with stretching the time at the beginning and ending of phrases.

WEEK 16

MON

Workout #106 **Type:** Scale **Sub-type:** G natural minor, G harmonic minor
Goals: 1) To develop an even, beautiful sound across the full range of the trumpet; 2) To reach the point in which you are no longer consciously thinking about the fingerings.
Tip: Start slowly and gradually increase the speed. Repeat the exercise a number of times until the fingerings become natural and subconscious.

TUE

Workout #107 **Type:** Articulation **Sub-type:** Contrasting
Goal: To play the different styles of articulation with contrast and beauty.
Tip: Exaggerate the difference between each type of articulation, while still keeping a beautiful sound.

WED

Workout #108 **Type:** Flexibility
Goal: To play relaxed, uninterrupted transitions between the partials of the trumpet.
Tip: Focus on the fact that you are simply playing one long steady stream of air. Imagining the sounds "tah" on lower notes and "ee" on upper notes may help move your air.

THU

Workout #109   **Type:** Interval   **Sub-type:** Pattern

Goal: To hear each interval in your head, and then to execute it through the trumpet.

Tip: Try singing these exercises to ensure that your ears are truly hearing each note.

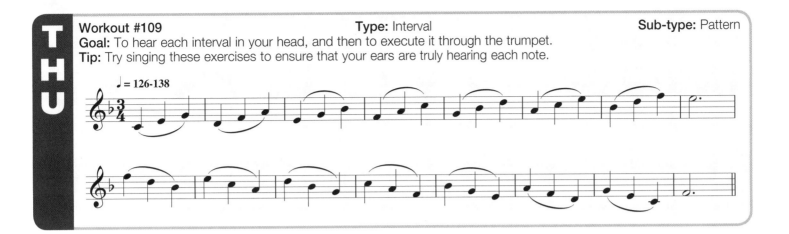

FRI

Workout #110   **Type:** Fingers   **Sub-type:** Third finger

Goal: To develop dexterity and control of the third finger.

Tip: Using the third finger feels awkward at first. Practice will promote the finger's independence.

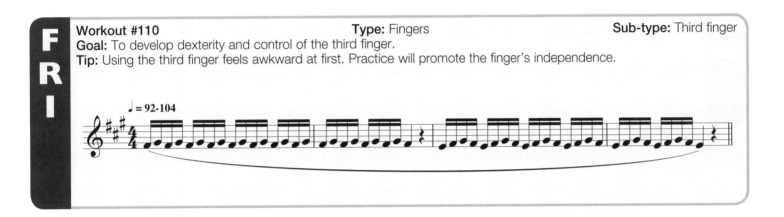

SAT

Workout #111   **Type:** Variety   **Sub-type:** Flow study

Goal: To produce an easy, connected, rich sound throughout the entire range of the trumpet.

Tip: Pretend that you are playing a single long tone with one long steady stream of air.

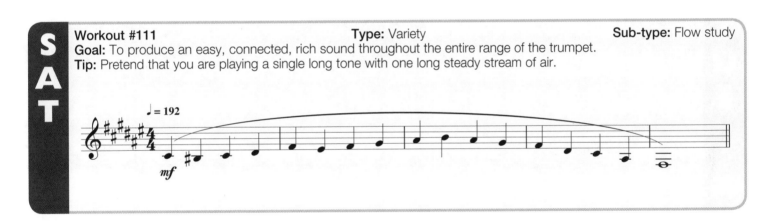

SUN

Workout #112   **Type:** Etude   **Sub-type:** G minor

Goal: To play musically and beautifully by utilizing the skills developed over the course of the week.

Tip: Listen to the audio track to formulate an idea of how you want to sound during the "Freely" section.

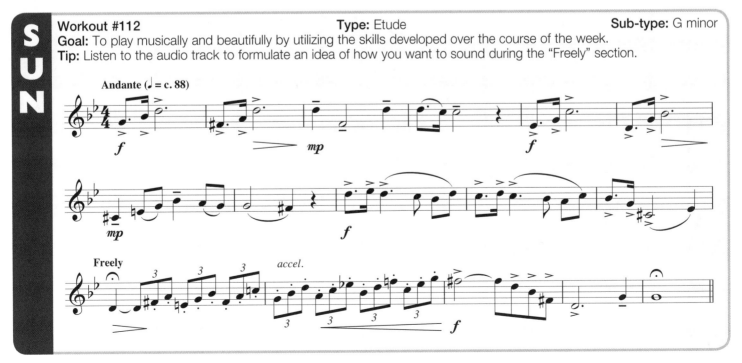

WEEK 17

MON

Workout #113   **Type:** Scale   **Sub-type:** B natural minor, B harmonic minor
Goals: 1) To develop an even, beautiful sound across the full range of the trumpet; 2) To reach the point in which you are no longer consciously thinking about the fingerings.
Tip: Start slowly and gradually increase the speed. Repeat the exercise a number of times until the fingerings become natural and subconscious.

natural minor   harmonic minor

TUE

Workout #114   **Type:** Articulation   **Sub-type:** Staccato
Goal: To produce a full-bodied tone that is detached from the other notes.
Tip: The notation of a tenuto together with a staccato means to play the note long but still separated.

WED

Workout #115   **Type:** Flexibility
Goal: To play relaxed, uninterrupted transitions between the partials of the trumpet.
Tip: Focus on the fact that you are simply playing one long steady stream of air. Imagining the sounds "tah" on lower notes and "ee" on upper notes may help move your air.

Workout #116   **Type:** Interval   **Sub-type:** Arpeggio

Goal: To hear each interval in your head, and then to execute it through the trumpet.

Tip: Try singing these exercises to ensure that your ears are truly hearing each note.

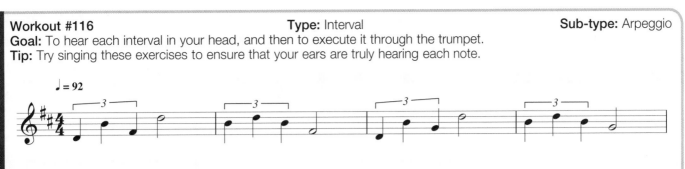

Workout #117   **Type:** Fingers   **Sub-type:** Third finger

Goal: To develop dexterity and control of the third finger.

Tip: Using the third finger feels awkward at first. Practice will promote the finger's independence.

Workout #118   **Type:** Variety   **Sub-type:** Upper register

Goal: To produce high notes that sound effortless without too much lip pressure or muscle strain.

Tip: Your focus should be on moving a fast, condensed stream of air. The notes may come out quietly at first. Volume will come as your embouchure gains muscle.

Workout #119   **Type:** Etude   **Sub-type:** B minor

Goal: To play musically and beautifully by utilizing the skills developed over the course of the week.

MON

Workout #120
Type: Scale **Sub-type:** C natural minor, C harmonic minor
Goals: 1) To develop an even, beautiful sound across the full range of the trumpet; 2) To reach the point in which you are no longer consciously thinking about the fingerings.
Tip: Start slowly and gradually increase the speed. Repeat the exercise a number of times until the fingerings become natural and subconscious.

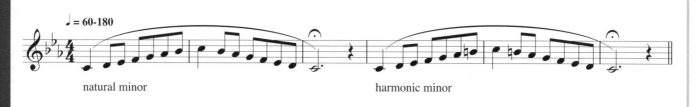

natural minor   harmonic minor

TUE

Workout #121
Type: Articulation **Sub-type:** Legato
Goal: To produce a pure tone that fluidly connects to the next note without a break.
Tip: Practice by imagining you are playing one single long tone, barely nicking the air to initiate each new note.

WED

Workout #122
Type: Flexibility
Goal: To play relaxed, uninterrupted transitions between the partials of the trumpet.
Tip: Focus on the fact that you are simply playing one long steady stream of air. Imagining the sounds "tah" on lower notes and "ee" on upper notes may help move your air.

THU

Workout #123 **Type:** Interval **Sub-type:** Expanding

Goal: To hear each interval in your head, and then to execute it through the trumpet.

Tip: Try singing these exercises to ensure that your ears are truly hearing each note. Imagine the wider intervals as being close together and easy to execute.

FRI

Workout #124 **Type:** Fingers **Sub-type:** Third finger

Goal: To develop dexterity and control of the third finger.

Tip: Using the third finger feels awkward at first. Practice will promote the finger's independence.

SAT

Workout #125 **Type:** Variety **Sub-type:** Upper register

Goal: To produce high notes that sound effortless without too much lip pressure or muscle strain.

Tip: Your focus should be on moving a fast, condensed stream of air. The notes may come out quietly at first. Volume will come as your embouchure gains muscle.

SUN

Workout #126 **Type:** Etude **Sub-type:** C minor

Goal: To play musically and beautifully by utilizing the skills developed over the course of the week.

WEEK 19

MON

Workout #127 **Type:** Scale **Sub-type:** F♯ natural minor, F♯ harmonic minor
Goals: 1) To develop an even, beautiful sound across the full range of the trumpet; 2) To reach the point in which you are no longer consciously thinking about the fingerings.
Tip: Start slowly and gradually increase the speed. Repeat the exercise a number of times until the fingerings become natural and subconscious.

natural minor harmonic minor

TUE

Workout #128 **Type:** Articulation **Sub-type:** Accent
Goal: To produce a strong, front-heavy articulation that is followed by a sustained and energized sound.
Tip: Keep the air moving in order to keep the sound activated throughout the entire duration of the note.

WED

Workout #129 **Type:** Flexibility
Goal: To play relaxed, uninterrupted transitions between the partials of the trumpet.
Tip: Focus on the fact that you are simply playing one long steady stream of air. Imagining the sounds "tah" on lower notes and "ee" on upper notes may help move your air.

THU

Workout #130   **Type:** Interval   **Sub-type:** Pattern

Goal: To hear each interval in your head, and then to execute it through the trumpet.
Tip: Try singing these exercises to ensure that your ears are truly hearing each note.

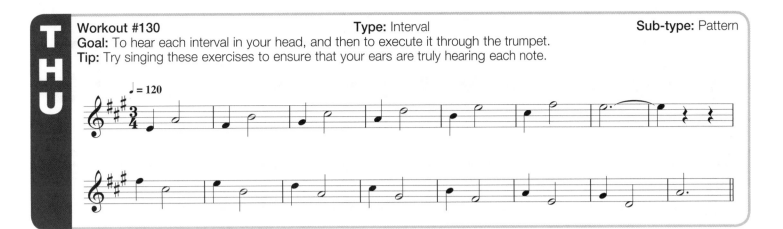

FRI

Workout #131   **Type:** Fingers   **Sub-type:** Third finger

Goal: To develop dexterity and control of the third finger.
Tip: Using the third finger feels awkward at first. Practice will promote the finger's independence.

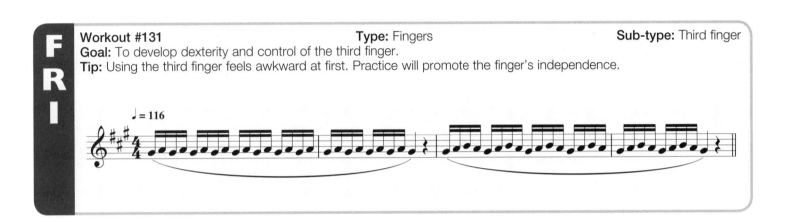

SAT

Workout #132   **Type:** Variety   **Sub-type:** Upper register

Goal: To produce high notes that sound effortless without too much lip pressure or muscle strain.
Tip: Your focus should be on moving a fast, condensed stream of air. The notes may come out quietly at first. Volume will come as your embouchure gains muscle.

SUN

Workout #133   **Type:** Etude   **Sub-type:** F# minor

Goal: To play musically and beautifully by utilizing the skills developed over the course of the week.
Tip: Challenge yourself to evoke a mysterious quality in the music.

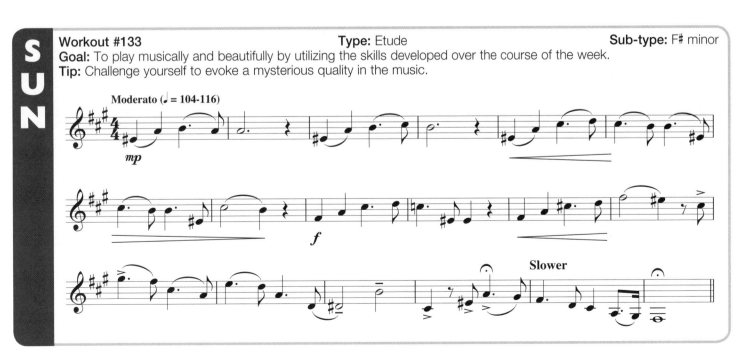

MON

Workout #134   **Type:** Scale   **Sub-type:** F natural minor, F harmonic minor
Goals: 1) To develop an even, beautiful sound across the full range of the trumpet; 2) To reach the point in which you are no longer consciously thinking about the fingerings.
Tip: Start slowly and gradually increase the speed. Repeat the exercise a number of times until the fingerings become natural and subconscious.

natural minor   harmonic minor

TUE

Workout #135   **Type:** Articulation   **Sub-type:** Legato
Goal: To produce a pure tone that fluidly connects to the next note without a break.
Tip: Practice by imagining you are playing one single long tone, barely nicking the air to initiate each new note.

WED

Workout #136   **Type:** Flexibility
Goal: To play relaxed, uninterrupted transitions between the partials of the trumpet.
Tip: Focus on the fact that you are simply playing one long steady stream of air. Imagining the sounds "tah" on lower notes and "ee" on upper notes may help move your air.

THU

Workout #137 **Type:** Interval **Sub-type:** Arpeggio

Goal: To hear each interval in your head, and then to execute it through the trumpet.

Tip: Try singing these exercises to ensure that your ears are truly hearing each note.

FRI

Workout #138 **Type:** Fingers **Sub-type:** Third finger

Goal: To develop dexterity and control of the third finger.

Tip: Using the third finger feels awkward at first. Practice will promote the finger's independence.

SAT

Workout #139 **Type:** Variety **Sub-type:** Upper register

Goal: To produce high notes that sound effortless without too much lip pressure or muscle strain.

Tip: Your focus should be on moving a fast, condensed stream of air. The notes may come out quietly at first. Volume will come as your embouchure gains muscle.

SUN

Workout #140 **Type:** Etude **Sub-type:** F minor

Goal: To play musically and beautifully by utilizing the skills developed over the course of the week.

Tip: Exaggerate the difference in character between the *mezzo-piano* and the *forte* passages.

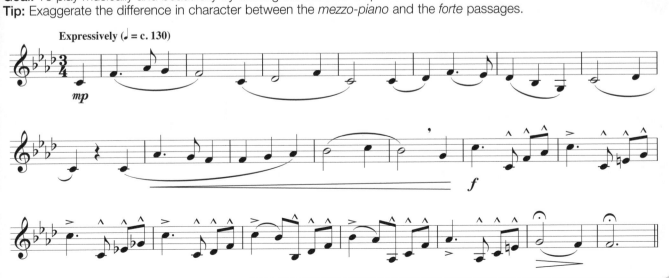

MON

Workout #141   **Type:** Scale   **Sub-type:** C# natural minor, C# harmonic minor

Goals: 1) To develop an even, beautiful sound across the full range of the trumpet; 2) To reach the point in which you are no longer consciously thinking about the fingerings.

Tip: Start slowly and gradually increase the speed. Repeat the exercise a number of times until the fingerings become natural and subconscious.

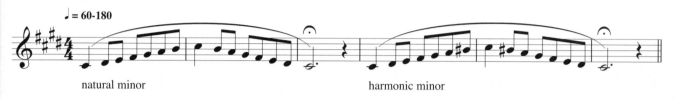

TUE

Workout #142   **Type:** Articulation   **Sub-type:** Staccato

Goal: To produce a full-bodied tone that is detached from the other notes.

Tip: Do not stop each note with your tongue. Let your air create the desired note length.

WED

Workout #143   **Type:** Flexibility

Goal: To play relaxed, uninterrupted transitions between the partials of the trumpet.

Tip: Focus on the fact that you are simply playing one long steady stream of air. Imagining the sounds "tah" on lower notes and "ee" on upper notes may help move your air.

THU

Workout #144   **Type:** Interval   **Sub-type:** Expanding

Goal: To hear each interval in your head, and then to execute it through the trumpet.

Tip: Try singing these exercises to ensure that your ears are truly hearing each note. Imagine the wider intervals as being close together and easy to execute.

FRI

Workout #145 **Type:** Fingers **Sub-type:** Third finger

Goal: To develop dexterity and control of the third finger.

Tip: Using the third finger feels awkward at first. Practice will promote the finger's independence.

SAT

Workout #146 **Type:** Variety **Sub-type:** Lip bends

Goals: 1) To lower the original pitch without valves by half a step while keeping a focused sound; 2) To find the "sweet spot" of the original note, the exact center where it vibrates with the most resonance.

Tip: Keep the embouchure firm; do not let it go completely loose. Strive to keep the bent note sound as similar in tone quality as possible to the original note.

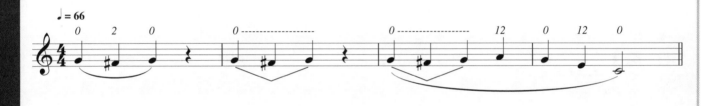

SUN

Workout #147 **Type:** Etude **Sub-type:** C# minor

Goal: To play musically and beautifully by utilizing the skills developed over the course of the week.

Tip: Emphasize the accents and dynamic shifts.

MON

Workout #148   **Type:** Scale   **Sub-type:** B♭ natural minor, B♭ harmonic minor
Goals: 1) To develop an even, beautiful sound across the full range of the trumpet; 2) To reach the point in which you are no longer consciously thinking about the fingerings.
Tip: Start slowly and gradually increase the speed. Repeat the exercise a number of times until the fingerings become natural and subconscious.

natural minor   harmonic minor

TUE

Workout #149   **Type:** Articulation   **Sub-type:** Marcato
Goal: To produce a strong, front-heavy articulation that is, generally speaking, shorter and more pointed than an accent.

WED

Workout #150   **Type:** Flexibility
Goal: To play relaxed, uninterrupted transitions between the partials of the trumpet.
Tip: Focus on the fact that you are simply playing one long steady stream of air. Imagining the sounds "tah" on lower notes and "ee" on upper notes may help move your air.

THU

Workout #151   **Type:** Interval   **Sub-type:** Pattern
Goal: To hear each interval in your head, and then to execute it through the trumpet.
Tip: Try singing these exercises to ensure that your ears are truly hearing each note.

FRI

Workout #152   **Type:** Fingers   **Sub-type:** Third finger

Goal: To develop dexterity and control of the third finger.

Tip: Using the third finger feels awkward at first. Practice will promote the finger's independence.

SAT

Workout #153   **Type:** Variety   **Sub-type:** Lip bends

Goals: 1) To lower the original pitch without valves by half a step while keeping a focused sound; 2) To find the "sweet spot" of the original note, the exact center where it vibrates with the most resonance.

Tip: Keep the embouchure firm; do not let it go completely loose. Strive to keep the bent note sound as similar in tone quality as possible to the original note.

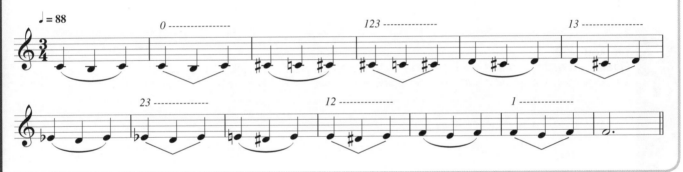

SUN

Workout #154   **Type:** Etude   **Sub-type:** B♭ minor, 4ths

Goal: To play musically and beautifully by utilizing the skills developed over the course of the week.

Tip: Strive for a full, resonant low register.

MON

Workout #155   **Type:** Scale   **Sub-type:** G♯ natural minor, G♯ harmonic minor
Goals: 1) To develop an even, beautiful sound across the full range of the trumpet; 2) To reach the point in which you are no longer consciously thinking about the fingerings.
Tip: Start slowly and gradually increase the speed. Repeat the exercise a number of times until the fingerings become natural and subconscious.
Note: The "✘" sign before a note is a double-sharp. Raise these notes by two half steps.

natural minor   harmonic minor

TUE

Workout #156   **Type:** Articulation   **Sub-type:** Legato
Goal: To produce a pure tone that fluidly connects to the next note without a break.
Tip: Practice by imagining you are playing one single long tone, barely nicking the air to initiate each new note.

WED

Workout #157   **Type:** Flexibility
Goal: To play relaxed, uninterrupted transitions between the partials of the trumpet.
Tip: Focus on the fact that you are simply playing one long steady stream of air. Imagining the sounds "tah" on lower notes and "ee" on upper notes may help move your air.

THU

Workout #158

Type: Interval **Sub-type:** Arpeggio

Goal: To hear each interval in your head, and then to execute it through the trumpet.

Tip: Try singing these exercises to ensure that your ears are truly hearing each note.

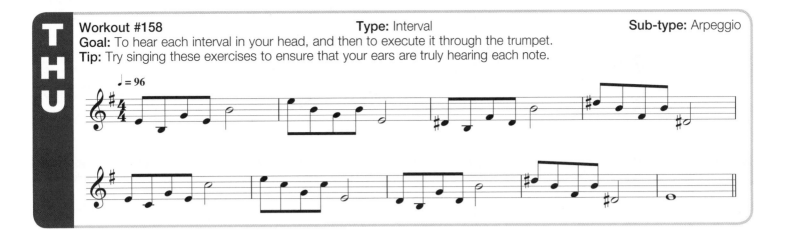

FRI

Workout #159

Type: Fingers **Sub-type:** Third finger

Goal: To develop dexterity and control of the third finger.

Tip: Using the third finger feels awkward at first. Practice will promote the finger's independence.

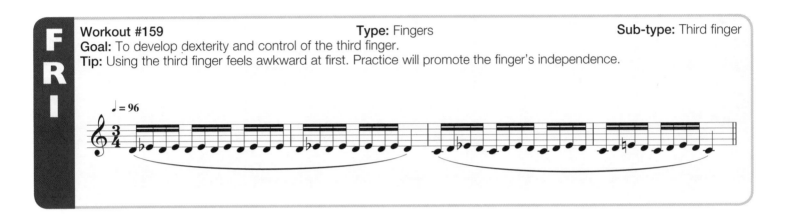

SAT

Workout #160

Type: Variety **Sub-type:** Lip bends

Goals: 1) To lower the original pitch without valves by half a step while keeping a focused sound; 2) To find the "sweet spot" of the original note, the exact center where it vibrates with the most resonance.

Tip: Keep the embouchure firm; do not let it go completely loose. Strive to keep the bent note sound as similar in tone quality as possible to the original note.

SUN

Workout #161

Type: Etude **Sub-type:** G# minor

Goal: To play musically and beautifully by utilizing the skills developed over the course of the week.

Tip: Experiment with stretching the time at the beginning and ending of phrases.

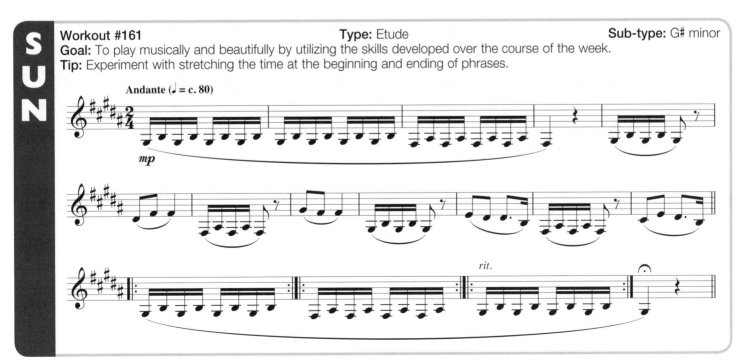

MON

Workout #162 **Type:** Scale **Sub-type:** E♭ natural minor, E♭ harmonic minor

Goals: 1) To develop an even, beautiful sound across the full range of the trumpet; 2) To reach the point in which you are no longer consciously thinking about the fingerings.

Tip: Start slowly and gradually increase the speed. Repeat the exercise a number of times until the fingerings become natural and subconscious.

TUE

Workout #163 **Type:** Articulation **Sub-type:** Staccato

Goal: To produce a full-bodied tone that is detached from the other notes.

Tip: Do not stop each note with your tongue. Let your air create the desired note length.

WED

Workout #164 **Type:** Flexibility

Goal: To play relaxed, uninterrupted transitions between the partials of the trumpet.

Tip: Focus on the fact that you are simply playing one long steady stream of air. Imagining the sounds "tah" on lower notes and "ee" on upper notes may help move your air.

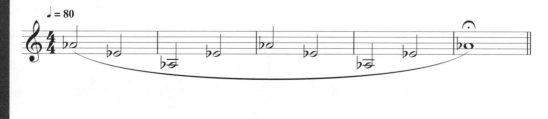

THU

Workout #165 **Type:** Interval **Sub-type:** Expanding

Goal: To hear each interval in your head, and then to execute it through the trumpet.

Tip: Try singing these exercises to ensure that your ears are truly hearing each note. Imagine the wider intervals as being close together and easy to execute.

FRI

Workout #166 **Type:** Fingers **Sub-type:** Third finger

Goal: To develop dexterity and control of the third finger.

Tip: Using the third finger feels awkward at first. Practice will promote the finger's independence.

SAT

Workout #167 **Type:** Variety **Sub-type:** Pedal register

Goals: 1) To produce a full and focused tone that is below the fingered range of the trumpet; 2) To have the sound be as similar in quality as possible to a fingered note.

Tip: Stay relaxed, be liberal with the use of warm, loose air. Do not set up a new embouchure to get the note to speak. Make sure you can move freely between the middle and pedal registers.

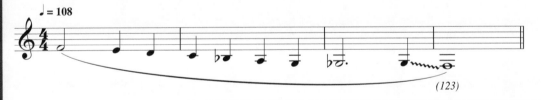

SUN

Workout #168 **Type:** Etude **Sub-type:** E♭ minor

Goal: To play musically and beautifully by utilizing the skills developed over the course of the week.

MON

Workout #169 **Type:** Scale **Sub-type:** A melodic minor
Goals: 1) To develop an even, beautiful sound across the full range of the trumpet; 2) To reach the point in which you are no longer consciously thinking about the fingerings.
Tip: Start slowly and gradually increase the speed. Repeat the exercise a number of times until the fingerings become natural and subconscious.

TUE

Workout #170 **Type:** Articulation **Sub-type:** Legato
Goal: To produce a pure tone that fluidly connects to the next note without a break.
Tip: Practice by imagining you are playing one single long tone, barely nicking the air to initiate each new note.

WED

Workout #171 **Type:** Flexibility
Goal: To play relaxed, uninterrupted transitions between the partials of the trumpet.
Tip: Focus on the fact that you are simply playing one long steady stream of air. Imagining the sounds "tah" on lower notes and "ee" on upper notes may help move your air.

THU

Workout #172 **Type:** Interval **Sub-type:** Pattern
Goal: To hear each interval in your head, and then to execute it through the trumpet.
Tip: Try singing these exercises to ensure that your ears are truly hearing each note.

Workout #173　　　　　　　　　**Type:** Fingers　　　　　　**Sub-type:** Chromatic full octave

Goal: To achieve agile, in-time, dexterous fingers.

Tip: Use a metronome and subdivide in your head. Every note should be perfectly in time.

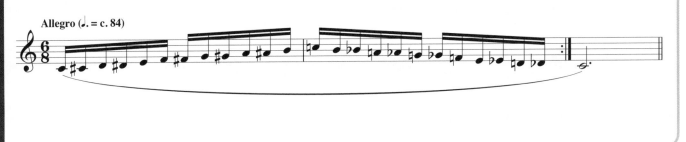

Workout #174　　　　　　　　　**Type:** Variety　　　　　　**Sub-type:** Pedal register

Goals: 1) To produce a full and focused tone that is below the fingered range of the trumpet; 2) To have the sound be as similar in quality as possible to a fingered note.

Tip: Stay relaxed, be liberal with the use of warm, loose air. Do not set up a new embouchure to get the note to speak. Make sure you can move freely between the middle and pedal registers.

Workout #175　　　　　　　　　**Type:** Etude　　　　　　**Sub-type:** A minor

Goal: To play musically and beautifully by utilizing the skills developed over the course of the week.

Tip: In order to be chant-like, play around with the time. Stretch certain notes, accelerate through others.

MON

Workout #176   **Type:** Scale   **Sub-type:** D melodic minor
Goals: 1) To develop an even, beautiful sound across the full range of the trumpet; 2) To reach the point in which you are no longer consciously thinking about the fingerings.
Tip: Start slowly and gradually increase the speed. Repeat the exercise a number of times until the fingerings become natural and subconscious.

TUE

Workout #177   **Type:** Articulation   **Sub-type:** Accent
Goal: To produce a strong, front-heavy articulation that is followed by a sustained and energized sound.
Tip: Keep the air moving in order to keep the sound activated throughout the entire duration of the note.

WED

Workout #178   **Type:** Flexibility
Goal: To play relaxed, uninterrupted transitions between the partials of the trumpet.
Tip: Focus on the fact that you are simply playing one long steady stream of air. Imagining the sounds "tah" on lower notes and "ee" on upper notes may help move your air.

THU

Workout #179 **Type:** Interval **Sub-type:** Arpeggio

Goal: To hear each interval in your head, and then to execute it through the trumpet.

Tip: Try singing these exercises to ensure that your ears are truly hearing each note.

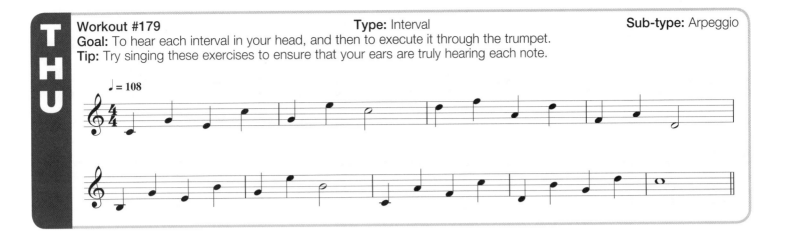

FRI

Workout #180 **Type:** Fingers **Sub-type:** Chromatic full octave

Goal: To achieve agile, in-time, dexterous fingers.

Tip: Use a metronome and subdivide in your head. Every note should be perfectly in time.

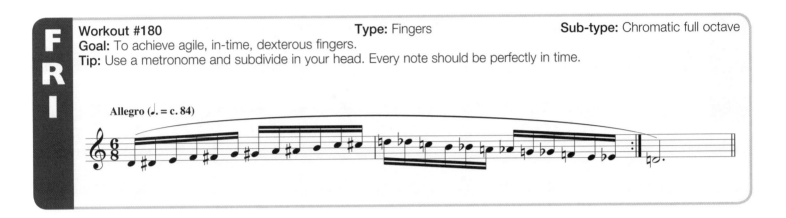

SAT

Workout #181 **Type:** Variety **Sub-type:** Pedal register

Goals: 1) To produce a full and focused tone that is below the fingered range of the trumpet; 2) To have the sound be as similar in quality as possible to a fingered note.

Tip: Stay relaxed, be liberal with the use of warm, loose air. Do not set up a new embouchure to get the note to speak. Make sure you can move freely between the middle and pedal registers.

SUN

Workout #182 **Type:** Etude **Sub-type:** D minor

Goal: To play musically and beautifully by utilizing the skills developed over the course of the week.

Tip: Keep the dotted-eighth/16th rhythm snappy.

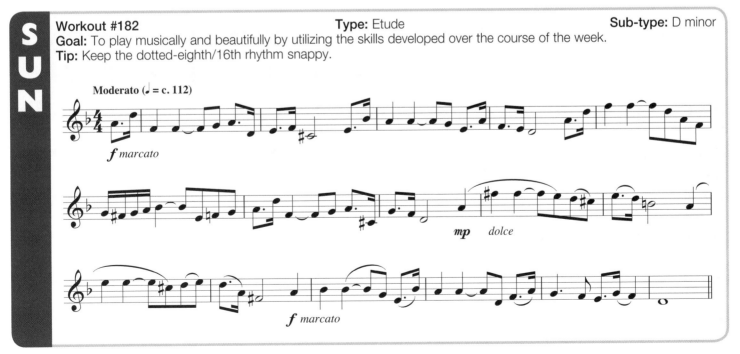

MON

Workout #183
Type: Scale   **Sub-type:** E melodic minor

Goals: 1) To develop an even, beautiful sound across the full range of the trumpet; 2) To reach the point in which you are no longer consciously thinking about the fingerings.

Tip: Start slowly and gradually increase the speed. Repeat the exercise a number of times until the fingerings become natural and subconscious.

TUE

Workout #184
Type: Articulation   **Sub-type:** Staccato

Goal: To produce a full-bodied tone that is detached from the other notes.

Tip: Do not stop each note with your tongue. Let your air create the desired note length.

WED

Workout #185
Type: Flexibility

Goal: To play relaxed, uninterrupted transitions between the partials of the trumpet.

Tip: Focus on the fact that you are simply playing one long steady stream of air. Imagining the sounds "tah" on lower notes and "ee" on upper notes may help move your air.

THU

Workout #186 **Type:** Interval **Sub-type:** Expanding

Goal: To hear each interval in your head, and then to execute it through the trumpet.

Tip: Try singing these exercises to ensure that your ears are truly hearing each note. Imagine the wider intervals as being close together and easy to execute.

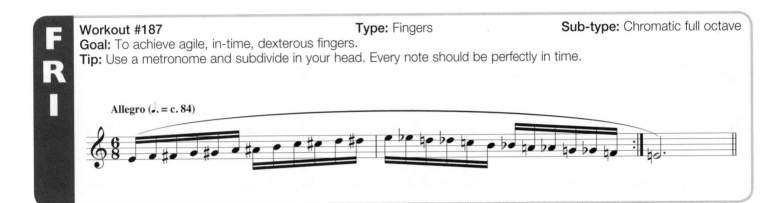

FRI

Workout #187 **Type:** Fingers **Sub-type:** Chromatic full octave

Goal: To achieve agile, in-time, dexterous fingers.

Tip: Use a metronome and subdivide in your head. Every note should be perfectly in time.

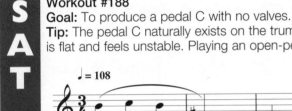

SAT

Workout #188 **Type:** Variety **Sub-type:** Pedal register

Goal: To produce a pedal C with no valves.

Tip: The pedal C naturally exists on the trumpet, but because of the straight-tubing nature of our instrument, the note is flat and feels unstable. Playing an open-pedal B first will help ease you into the C. Use plenty of warm air.

SUN

Workout #189 **Type:** Etude **Sub-type:** E minor

Goal: To play musically and beautifully by utilizing the skills developed over the course of the week.

MON

Workout #190
Type: Scale   **Sub-type:** G melodic minor
Goals: 1) To develop an even, beautiful sound across the full range of the trumpet; 2) To reach the point in which you are no longer consciously thinking about the fingerings.
Tip: Start slowly and gradually increase the speed. Repeat the exercise a number of times until the fingerings become natural and subconscious.

TUE

Workout #191
Type: Articulation   **Sub-type:** Legato
Goal: To produce a pure tone that fluidly connects to the next note without a break.
Tip: The legato notes should feel almost exactly the same as the slurred notes. The only difference is the addition a gentle tongue, barely nicking the air.

WED

Workout #192
Type: Flexibility
Goal: To play relaxed, uninterrupted transitions between the partials of the trumpet.
Tip: Focus on the fact that you are simply playing one long steady stream of air. Imagining the sounds "tah" on lower notes and "ee" on upper notes may help move your air.

THU

Workout #193 **Type:** Interval **Sub-type:** Pattern
Goal: To hear each interval in your head, and then to execute it through the trumpet.
Tip: Try singing these exercises to ensure that your ears are truly hearing each note.

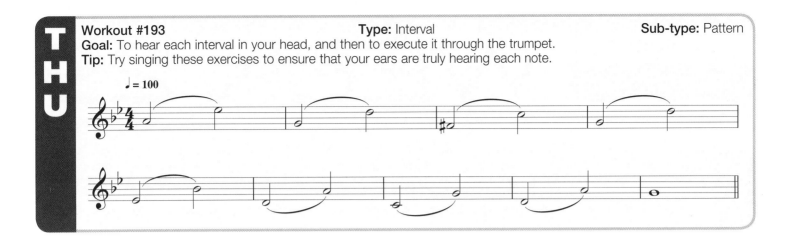

FRI

Workout #194 **Type:** Fingers **Sub-type:** Chromatic full octave
Goal: To achieve agile, in-time, dexterous fingers.
Tip: Use a metronome and subdivide in your head. Every note should be perfectly in time.

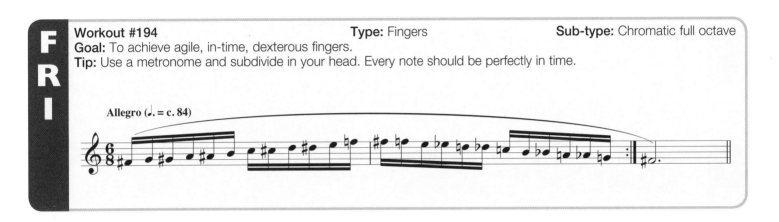

SAT

Workout #195 **Type:** Variety **Sub-type:** Upper register
Goal: To produce high notes that sound effortless without too much lip pressure or muscle strain.
Tip: Your focus should be on moving a fast, condensed stream of air. The notes may come out quietly at first. Volume will come as your embouchure gains muscle.

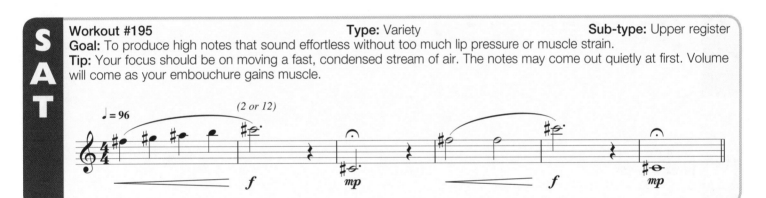

SUN

Workout #196 **Type:** Etude **Sub-type:** G minor
Goal: To play musically and beautifully by utilizing the skills developed over the course of the week.
Tip: Experiment with the use of rubato by slightly lengthening the first note of the 16th-note passages.

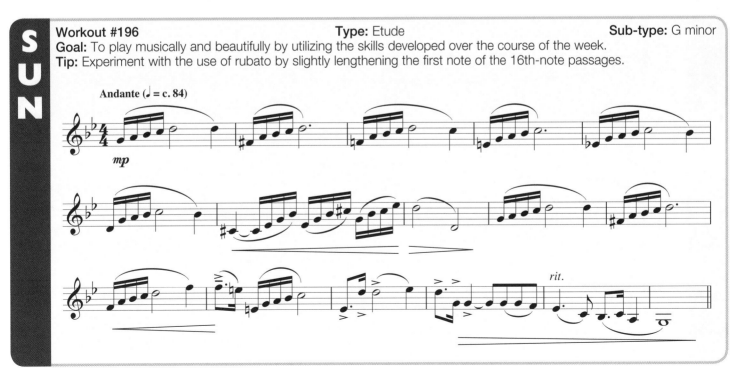

MON

Workout #197 **Type:** Scale **Sub-type:** B melodic minor

Goals: 1) To develop an even, beautiful sound across the full range of the trumpet; 2) To reach the point in which you are no longer consciously thinking about the fingerings.

Tip: Start slowly and gradually increase the speed. Repeat the exercise a number of times until the fingerings become natural and subconscious.

TUE

Workout #198 **Type:** Articulation **Sub-type:** Marcato vs. Accent

Goal: To exaggerate the contrast between *marcato* and accented articulations.

Tip: Accents are sustained, *marcatos* are more pointed.

WED

Workout #199 **Type:** Flexibility

Goal: To play relaxed, uninterrupted transitions between the partials of the trumpet.

Tip: Focus on the fact that you are simply playing one long steady stream of air. Imagining the sounds "tah" on lower notes and "ee" on upper notes may help move your air.

THU

Workout #200 **Type:** Interval **Sub-type:** Arpeggio

Goal: To hear each interval in your head, and then to execute it through the trumpet.

Tip: Try singing these exercises to ensure that your ears are truly hearing each note.

FRI

Workout #201 **Type:** Fingers **Sub-type:** Chromatic full octave
Goal: To achieve agile, in-time, dexterous fingers.
Tip: Use a metronome and subdivide in your head. Every note should be perfectly in time.

SAT

Workout #202 **Type:** Variety **Sub-type:** Upper register
Goal: To produce high notes that sound effortless without too much lip pressure or muscle strain.
Tip: Your focus should be on moving a fast, condensed stream of air. The notes may come out quietly at first. Volume will come as your embouchure gains muscle.

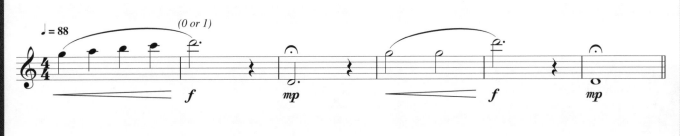

SUN

Workout #203 **Type:** Etude **Sub-type:** B minor
Goal: To play musically and beautifully by utilizing the skills developed over the course of the week.
Tip: Keep the sound and air flowing to produce long, lyrical lines.

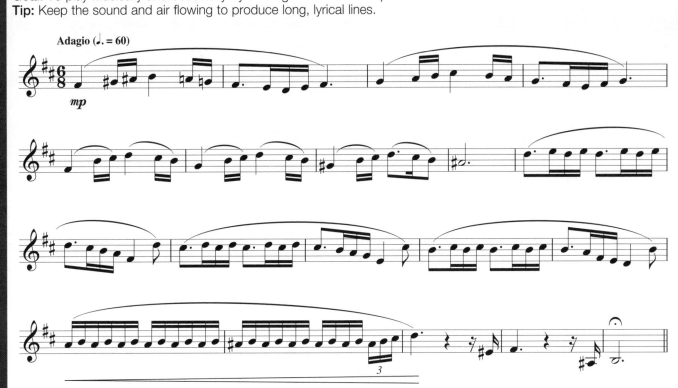

WEEK 30

MON

Workout #204   Type: Scale   Sub-type: C melodic minor

Goals: 1) To develop an even, beautiful sound across the full range of the trumpet; 2) To reach the point in which you are no longer consciously thinking about the fingerings.

Tip: Start slowly and gradually increase the speed. Repeat the exercise a number of times until the fingerings become natural and subconscious.

TUE

Workout #205   Type: Articulation   Sub-type: Staccatissimo

Goal: To produce a very short, yet still full-bodied tone.

Tip: Try to pack as much sound as possible into the short duration of each note.

WED

Workout #206   Type: Flexibility

Goal: To play relaxed, uninterrupted transitions between the partials of the trumpet.

Tip: Focus on the fact that you are simply playing one long steady stream of air. Imagining the sounds "tah" on lower notes and "ee" on upper notes may help move your air.

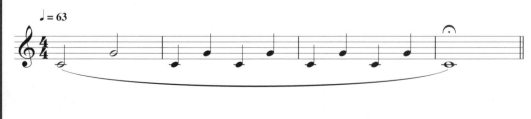

THU

Workout #207

Type: Interval   **Sub-type:** Expanding

Goal: To hear each interval in your head, and then to execute it through the trumpet.

Tip: Try singing these exercises to ensure that your ears are truly hearing each note. Imagine the wider intervals as being close together and easy to execute.

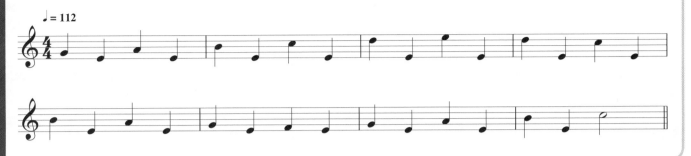

FRI

Workout #208

Type: Fingers   **Sub-type:** Chromatic full octave

Goal: To achieve agile, in-time, dexterous fingers.

Tip: Use a metronome and subdivide in your head. Every note should be perfectly in time.

SAT

Workout #209

Type: Variety   **Sub-type:** Ornaments – grace notes

Goal: To produce a graceful, musical, and natural-sounding embellishment.

Tip: Start slowly and deliberately. The end result should be a quick, playful gesture.

SUN

Workout #210

Type: Etude   **Sub-type:** C minor

Goal: To play musically and beautifully by utilizing the skills developed over the course of the week.

Tip: Play dramatically. This etude should sound reminiscent of a film score.

MON

Workout #211 **Type:** Scale **Sub-type:** F# melodic minor
Goals: 1) To develop an even, beautiful sound across the full range of the trumpet; 2) To reach the point in which you are no longer consciously thinking about the fingerings.
Tip: Start slowly and gradually increase the speed. Repeat the exercise a number of times until the fingerings become natural and subconscious.

TUE

Workout #212 **Type:** Articulation **Sub-type:** Legato
Goal: To produce a pure tone that fluidly connects to the next note without a break.
Tip: Practice by imagining you are playing one single long tone, barely nicking the air to initiate each new note.

WED

Workout #213 **Type:** Flexibility
Goal: To play relaxed, uninterrupted transitions between the partials of the trumpet.
Tip: Focus on the fact that you are simply playing one long steady stream of air. Imagining the sounds "tah" on lower notes and "ee" on upper notes may help move your air.

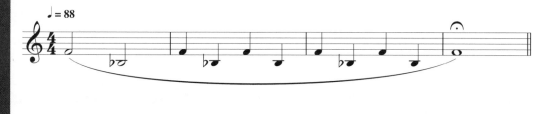

THU

Workout #214 **Type:** Interval **Sub-type:** Pattern

Goal: To hear each interval in your head, and then to execute it through the trumpet.

Tip: Try singing these exercises to ensure that your ears are truly hearing each note.

FRI

Workout #215 **Type:** Fingers **Sub-type:** Chromatic full octave

Goal: To achieve agile, in-time, dexterous fingers.

Tip: Use a metronome and subdivide in your head. Every note should be perfectly in time.

SAT

Workout #216 **Type:** Variety **Sub-type:** Ornaments – grace notes

Goal: To produce a graceful, musical, and natural-sounding embellishment.

Tip: Start slowly and deliberately. The end result should be a quick, playful gesture.

SUN

Workout #217 **Type:** Etude **Sub-type:** F# minor

Goal: To play musically and beautifully by utilizing the skills developed over the course of the week.

Tip: Keep the grace notes quick and snappy, but not rushed or hectic.

MON

Workout #218 **Type:** Scale **Sub-type:** F melodic minor
Goals: 1) To develop an even, beautiful sound across the full range of the trumpet; 2) To reach the point in which you are no longer consciously thinking about the fingerings.
Tip: Start slowly and gradually increase the speed. Repeat the exercise a number of times until the fingerings become natural and subconscious.

TUE

Workout #219 **Type:** Articulation **Sub-type:** Staccato
Goal: To produce a full-bodied tone that is detached from the other notes.
Tip: Do not stop each note with your tongue. Let your air create the desired note length.

WED

Workout #220 **Type:** Flexibility
Goal: To play relaxed, uninterrupted transitions between the partials of the trumpet.
Tip: Focus on the fact that you are simply playing one long steady stream of air. Imagining the sounds "tah" on lower notes and "ee" on upper notes may help move your air.

THU

Workout #221 **Type:** Interval **Sub-type:** Arpeggio
Goal: To hear each interval in your head, and then to execute it through the trumpet.
Tip: Try singing these exercises to ensure that your ears are truly hearing each note.

FRI

Workout #222   **Type:** Fingers   **Sub-type:** Agility
Goal: To achieve agile, in-time, dexterous fingers.
Tip: Use a metronome and subdivide in your head. Every note should be perfectly in time.

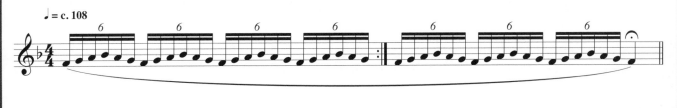

SAT

Workout #223   **Type:** Variety   **Sub-type:** Ornaments – grace notes
Goal: To produce a graceful, musical, and natural-sounding embellishment.
Tip: Start slowly and deliberately. The end result should be a quick, playful gesture.

SUN

Workout #224   **Type:** Etude   **Sub-type:** F minor
Goal: To play musically and beautifully by utilizing the skills developed over the course of the week.
Tip: Strive to keep the grace notes as part of the musical line instead of overly emphasizing them.

MON

Workout #225 **Type:** Scale **Sub-type:** C# melodic minor
Goals: 1) To develop an even, beautiful sound across the full range of the trumpet; 2) To reach the point in which you are no longer consciously thinking about the fingerings.
Tip: Start slowly and gradually increase the speed. Repeat the exercise a number of times until the fingerings become natural and subconscious.

TUE

Workout #226 **Type:** Articulation **Sub-type:** Accent
Goal: To produce a strong, front-heavy articulation that is followed by a sustained and energized sound.
Tip: Keep the air moving in order to keep the sound activated throughout the entire duration of the note.

WED

Workout #227 **Type:** Flexibility
Goal: To play relaxed, uninterrupted transitions between the partials of the trumpet.
Tip: Focus on the fact that you are simply playing one long steady stream of air. Imagining the sounds "tah" on lower notes and "ee" on upper notes may help move your air.

Workout #228 **Type:** Interval **Sub-type:** Expanding

Goal: To hear each interval in your head, and then to execute it through the trumpet.

Tip: Try singing these exercises to ensure that your ears are truly hearing each note. Imagine the wider intervals as being close together and easy to execute.

FRI

Workout #229 **Type:** Fingers **Sub-type:** Agility

Goal: To achieve agile, in-time, dexterous fingers.

Tip: Use a metronome and subdivide in your head. Every note should be perfectly in time.

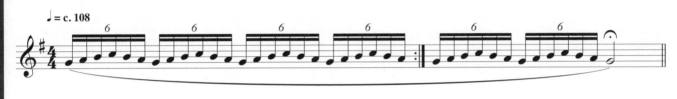

SAT

Workout #230 **Type:** Variety **Sub-type:** Ornaments – grace notes

Goal: To produce a graceful, musical, and natural-sounding embellishment.

Tip: Start slowly and deliberately. The end result should be a quick, playful gesture.

SUN

Workout #231 **Type:** Etude **Sub-type:** C# minor

Goal: To play musically and beautifully by utilizing the skills developed over the course of the week.

Tip: Imagine the sound of the flute and how sinuously they can play grace notes in this context.

MON

Workout #232   **Type:** Scale   **Sub-type:** B♭ melodic minor
Goals: 1) To develop an even, beautiful sound across the full range of the trumpet; 2) To reach the point in which you are no longer consciously thinking about the fingerings.
Tip: Start slowly and gradually increase the speed. Repeat the exercise a number of times until the fingerings become natural and subconscious.

TUE

Workout #233   **Type:** Articulation   **Sub-type:** Legato
Goal: To produce a pure tone that fluidly connects to the next note without a break.
Tip: Practice by imagining you are playing one single long tone, barely nicking the air to initiate each new note.

WED

Workout #234   **Type:** Flexibility
Goal: To play relaxed, uninterrupted transitions between the partials of the trumpet.
Tip: Focus on the fact that you are simply playing one long steady stream of air. Imagining the sounds "tah" on lower notes and "ee" on upper notes may help move your air.

THU

Workout #235   **Type:** Interval   **Sub-type:** Pattern

Goal: To hear each interval in your head, and then to execute it through the trumpet.

Tip: Try singing these exercises to ensure that your ears are truly hearing each note.

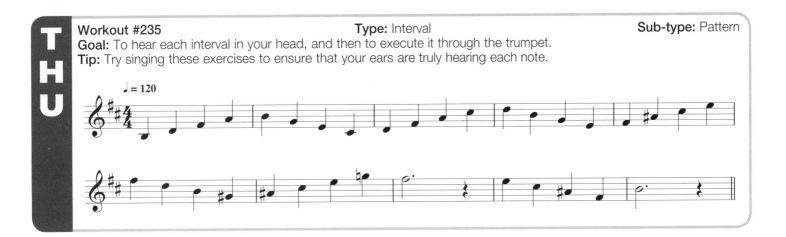

FRI

Workout #236   **Type:** Fingers   **Sub-type:** Agility

Goal: To achieve agile, in-time, dexterous fingers.

Tip: Use a metronome and subdivide in your head. Every note should be perfectly in time.

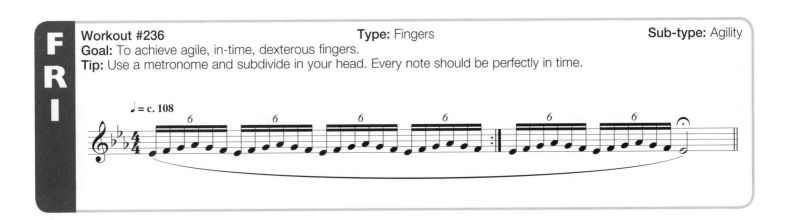

SAT

Workout #237   **Type:** Variety   **Sub-type:** Ornaments – trills

Goal: To produce a graceful, musical, and natural-sounding embellishment.

Tip: Keep your air moving and aim it for the middle of the two pitches.

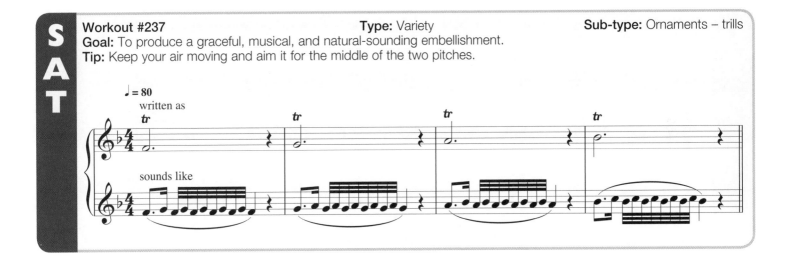

SUN

Workout #238   **Type:** Etude   **Sub-type:** B♭ minor

Goal: To play musically and beautifully by utilizing the skills developed over the course of the week.

Note: A trill sign with a flat above it instructs you to lower the trilled upper note by a half step. Likewise, a trill sign with a sharp above it instructs you to raise the upper note by a half step.

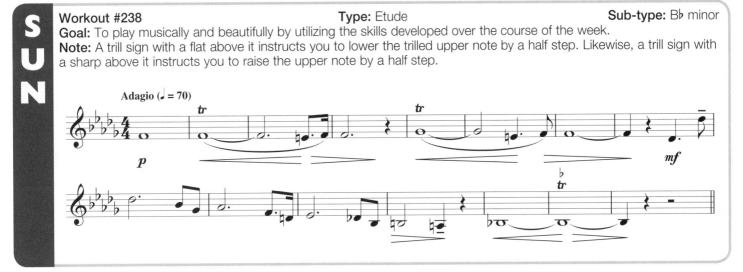

73

WEEK 35

MON

Workout #239 **Type:** Scale **Sub-type:** G# melodic minor

Goals: 1) To develop an even, beautiful sound across the full range of the trumpet; 2) To reach the point in which you are no longer consciously thinking about the fingerings.

Tip: Start slowly and gradually increase the speed. Repeat the exercise a number of times until the fingerings become natural and subconscious.

TUE

Workout #240 **Type:** Articulation **Sub-type:** Accent

Goal: To produce a strong, front-heavy articulation that is followed by a sustained and energized sound.

Tip: Keep the air moving in order to keep the sound activated throughout the entire duration of the note.

WED

Workout #241 **Type:** Flexibility

Goal: To play relaxed, uninterrupted transitions between the partials of the trumpet.

Tip: Focus on the fact that you are simply playing one long steady stream of air. Imagining the sounds "tah" on lower notes and "ee" on upper notes may help move your air.

THU

Workout #242　　　　　　　　　　　**Type:** Interval　　　　　　　　　　　**Sub-type:** Arpeggio

Goal: To hear each interval in your head, and then to execute it through the trumpet.

Tip: Try singing these exercises to ensure that your ears are truly hearing each note.

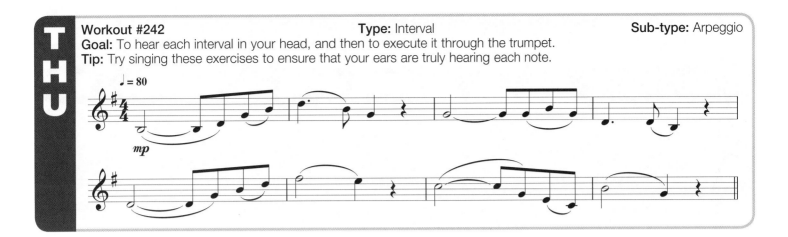

FRI

Workout #243　　　　　　　　　　　**Type:** Fingers　　　　　　　　　　　**Sub-type:** Agility

Goal: To achieve agile, in-time, dexterous fingers.

Tip: Use a metronome and subdivide in your head. Every note should be perfectly in time.

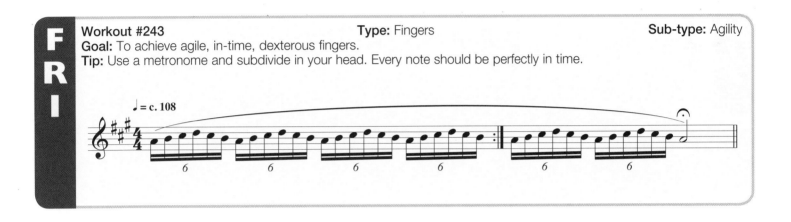

SAT

Workout #244　　　　　　　　　　　**Type:** Variety　　　　　　　　　　　**Sub-type:** Ornaments – trills

Goal: To produce a graceful, musical, and natural-sounding embellishment.

Tip: Practice exiting the trill slowly and deliberately at first to stick the landing.

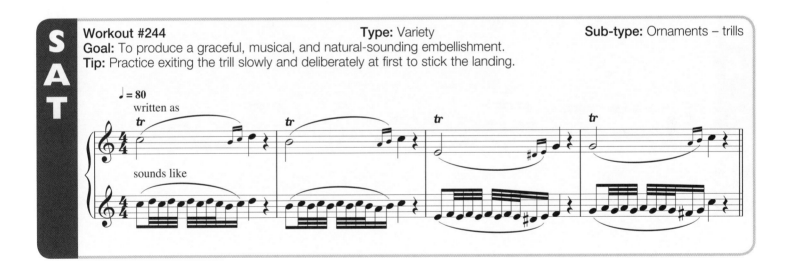

SUN

Workout #245　　　　　　　　　　　**Type:** Etude　　　　　　　　　　　**Sub-type:** G# minor

Goal: To play musically and beautifully by utilizing the skills developed over the course of the week.

Tip: Challenge yourself to keep the trills clean and, in the fifth and sixth measures, to connect the octave leaps.

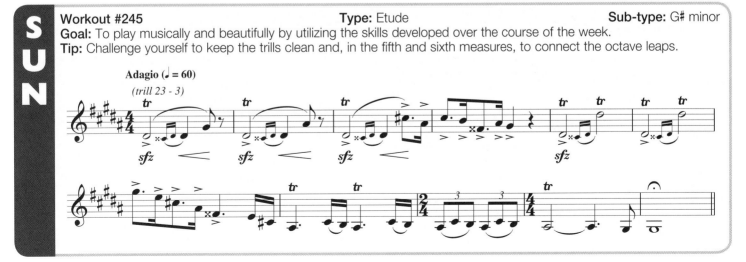

MON

Workout #246 **Type:** Scale **Sub-type:** E♭ melodic minor

Goals: 1) To develop an even, beautiful sound across the full range of the trumpet; 2) To reach the point in which you are no longer consciously thinking about the fingerings.

Tip: Start slowly and gradually increase the speed. Repeat the exercise a number of times until the fingerings become natural and subconscious.

TUE

Workout #247 **Type:** Articulation **Sub-type:** Staccato

Goal: To produce a full-bodied tone that is detached from the other notes.

Tip: Do not stop each note with your tongue. Let your air create the desired note length.

WED

Workout #248 **Type:** Flexibility

Goal: To play relaxed, uninterrupted transitions between the partials of the trumpet.

Tip: Focus on the fact that you are simply playing one long steady stream of air. Imagining the sounds "tah" on lower notes and "ee" on upper notes may help move your air.

THU

Workout #249   Type: Interval   Sub-type: Expanding

Goal: To hear each interval in your head, and then to execute it through the trumpet.
Tip: Add weight each marcato note, using it as a springboard to reach the next note.

FRI

Workout #250   Type: Fingers   Sub-type: Agility

Goal: To achieve agile, in-time, dexterous fingers.
Tip: Use a metronome and subdivide in your head. Every note should be perfectly in time.

SAT

Workout #251   Type: Variety   Sub-type: Ornaments – trills

Goal: To produce a graceful, musical, and natural-sounding embellishment.
Note: This kind of notation is usually reserved for trills between wider intervals. The two whole notes are happening simultaneously, so despite what it might look like, there are only four beats in each measure.

SUN

Workout #252   Type: Etude   Sub-type: E♭ minor

Goal: To play musically and beautifully by utilizing the skills developed over the course of the week.
Tip: Keep the dotted-eighth/16th rhythms snappy.

WEEK 37

MON

Workout #253   **Type:** Scale   **Sub-type:** C, D, E, F♯, A♭, B♭ whole tone
Goals: 1) To develop an even, beautiful sound across the full range of the trumpet; 2) To reach the point in which you are no longer consciously thinking about the fingerings.
Note: This scale is symmetrical, meaning that the intervals between pitches are all the same. Because of this, the scales listed in the Sub-type share the same notes. Basically, you are learning six whole tone scales at once.

TUE

Workout #254   **Type:** Articulation   **Sub-type:** Legato
Goal: To produce a pure tone that fluidly connects to the next note without a break.
Tip: Practice by imagining you are playing one single long tone, barely nicking the air to initiate each new note.

WED

Workout #255   **Type:** Flexibility
Goal: To play relaxed, uninterrupted transitions between the partials of the trumpet.
Tip: Focus on the fact that you are simply playing one long steady stream of air. Imagining the sounds "tah" on lower notes and "ee" on upper notes may help move your air.

THU

Workout #256   **Type:** Interval   **Sub-type:** Pattern
Goal: To hear each interval in your head, and then to execute it through the trumpet.
Tip: Try singing these exercises to ensure that your ears are truly hearing each note.

Workout #257 **Type:** Fingers **Sub-type:** Chromatic whole steps

Goal: To achieve agile, in-time, dexterous fingers.

Tip: Use a metronome and subdivide in your head. Every note should be perfectly in time.

Workout #258 **Type:** Variety **Sub-type:** Ornaments – alternate fingering trills

Goal: To produce a graceful, musical, and natural-sounding embellishment.

Tip: Knowing the trumpet's alternate fingerings (shown in the fingering chart on page 5) will make the majority of awkward trills easier.

Note: A trill sign with a flat above it instructs you to lower the trilled upper note by a half step. Likewise, a trill sign with a sharp above it instructs you to raise the upper note by a half step.

Workout #259 **Type:** Etude **Sub-type:** D whole tone

Goal: To play musically and beautifully by utilizing the skills developed over the course of the week.

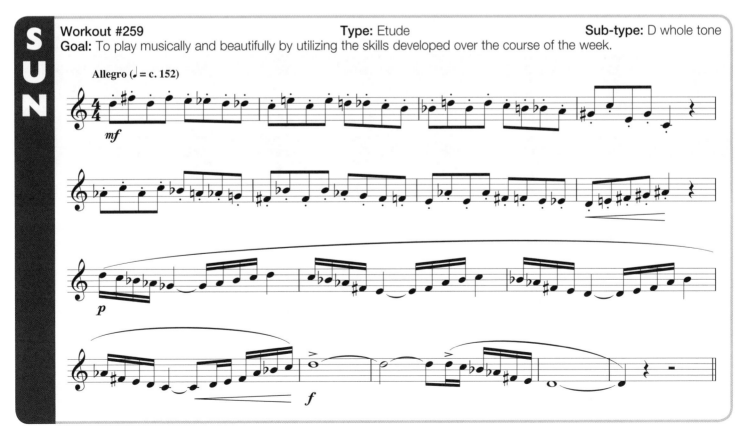

MON

Workout #260 **Type:** Scale **Sub-type:** C#, D#, F, G, A, B whole tone

Goals: 1) To develop an even, beautiful sound across the full range of the trumpet; 2) To reach the point in which you are no longer consciously thinking about the fingerings.

Note: This scale is symmetrical, meaning that the intervals between pitches are all the same. Because of this, the scales listed in the Sub-type share the same notes. Basically, you are learning six whole tone scales at once.

TUE

Workout #261 **Type:** Articulation **Sub-type:** Staccato

Goal: To produce a full-bodied tone that is detached from the other notes.

Tip: Do not stop each note with your tongue. Let your air create the desired note length.

WED

Workout #262 **Type:** Flexibility

Goal: To play relaxed, uninterrupted transitions between the partials of the trumpet.

Tip: Focus on the fact that you are simply playing one long steady stream of air. Imagining the sounds "tah" on lower notes and "ee" on upper notes may help move your air.

THU

Workout #263 **Type:** Interval **Sub-type:** Arpeggio

Goal: To hear each interval in your head, and then to execute it through the trumpet.

Tip: Try singing these exercises to ensure that your ears are truly hearing each note.

Workout #264   **Type:** Fingers   **Sub-type:** Chromatic whole steps

Goal: To achieve agile, in-time, dexterous fingers.

Tip: Use a metronome and subdivide in your head. Every note should be perfectly in time.

Workout #265   **Type:** Variety   **Sub-type:** Ornaments – turns

Goal: To produce a graceful, musical, and natural-sounding embellishment.

Tip: The "S" symbol is a turn. Play one note above the given pitch, then the original pitch, then one note below it, then the original pitch again, as shown in the lower staff.

Note: You may see the "S" turn sign flipped around. In this case, play the lower note first, then the upper note.

Workout #266   **Type:** Etude   **Sub-type:** F whole tone

Goal: To play musically and beautifully by utilizing the skills developed over the course of the week.

Tip: Challenge yourself to be even more expressive.

MON

Workout #267 **Type:** Scale **Sub-type:** C Mixolydian

Goals: 1) To develop an even, beautiful sound across the full range of the trumpet; 2) To reach the point in which you are no longer consciously thinking about the fingerings.

Note: A Mixolydian scale can be thought of as a major scale with a lowered 7th.

TUE

Workout #268 **Type:** Articulation **Sub-type:** Legato, accent

Goal: To play the contrasting legato and accented passages beautifully.

Tip: Although there are contrasting articulations, treat the line as one single musical idea.

WED

Workout #269 **Type:** Flexibility

Goal: To play relaxed, uninterrupted transitions between the partials of the trumpet.

Tip: Focus on the fact that you are simply playing one long steady stream of air. Imagining the sounds "tah" on lower notes and "ee" on upper notes may help move your air.

THU

Workout #270 **Type:** Interval **Sub-type:** Expanding

Goal: To hear each interval in your head, and then to execute it through the trumpet.

Tip: Try singing these exercises to ensure that your ears are truly hearing each note. Imagine the wider intervals as being close together and easy to execute.

Workout #271   **Type:** Fingers   **Sub-type:** Chromatic whole steps

Goal: To achieve agile, in-time, dexterous fingers.

Tip: Use a metronome and subdivide in your head. Every note should be perfectly in time.

Workout #272   **Type:** Variety   **Sub-type:** Ornaments – mordents

Goal: To produce a graceful, musical, and natural-sounding embellishment.

Tip: The mordent symbol tells you to play the written note, one note above, and then the written note again, rapidly at the beginning of the given pitch. If the mordent symbol has a slash through it, do the same thing, but with one note below instead of above.

Workout #273   **Type:** Etude   **Sub-type:** D Mixolydian

Goal: To play musically and beautifully by utilizing the skills developed over the course of the week.

Tip: Don't be afraid to be pompous and boisterous with this one.

MON

Workout #274 **Type:** Scale **Sub-type:** C Dorian

Goals: 1) To develop an even, beautiful sound across the full range of the trumpet; 2) To reach the point in which you are no longer consciously thinking about the fingerings.

Note: A Dorian scale can be thought of as a natural minor scale with a raised scale degree 6.

TUE

Workout #275 **Type:** Articulation **Sub-type:** Contrast

Goal: To play four distinct types of articulations.

Tip: Exaggerate the differences between these four articulations

WED

Workout #276 **Type:** Flexibility

Goal: To play relaxed, uninterrupted transitions between the partials of the trumpet.

Tip: Focus on the fact that you are simply playing one long steady stream of air. Imagining the sounds "tah" on lower notes and "ee" on upper notes may help move your air.

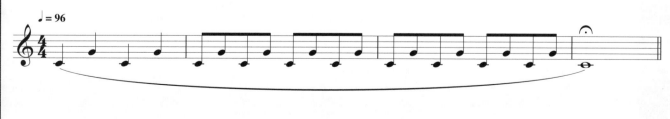

Workout #277　　　　　　**Type:** Interval　　　　　　**Sub-type:** Pattern

Goal: To hear each interval in your head, and then to execute it through the trumpet.

Tip: Try singing these exercises to ensure that your ears are truly hearing each note.

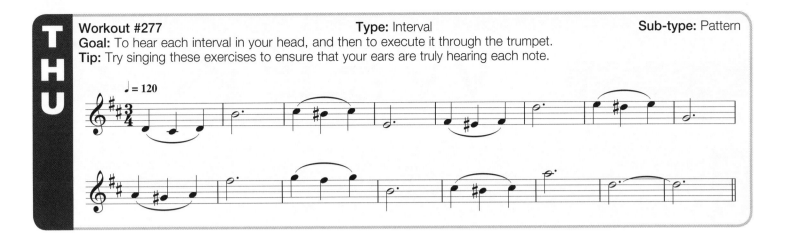

Workout #278　　　　　　**Type:** Fingers　　　　　　**Sub-type:** Chromatic whole steps

Goal: To achieve agile, in-time, dexterous fingers.

Tip: Use a metronome and subdivide in your head. Every note should be perfectly in time.

Workout #279　　　　　　**Type:** Variety　　　　　　**Sub-type:** Effects – falls

Goal: To fall off of a note in the jazz/commercial style.

Tip: There are a few different ways to play falls. For this example, wiggle the valves as you are dropping off the note. Listen to the big bands listed on page 4 use this technique and copy what you hear.

Workout #280　　　　　　**Type:** Etude　　　　　　**Sub-type:** C Dorian

Goal: To play musically and beautifully by utilizing the skills developed over the course of the week.

Tip: Internalize the sound of the A♮s in this etude. This note, scale degree 6, carries the defining sound of the Dorian mode.

MON

Workout #281 **Type:** Scale **Sub-type:** C Lydian
Goals: 1) To develop an even, beautiful sound across the full range of the trumpet; 2) To reach the point in which you are no longer consciously thinking about the fingerings.
Note: A Lydian scale can be thought of as a major scale with a raised 4th.

TUE

Workout #282 **Type:** Articulation **Sub-type:** Accent, marcato
Goal: To play both types of front-heavy articulations with strength.
Tip: Make sure that even the quick notes have a full body of sound.

WED

Workout #283 **Type:** Flexibility
Goal: To play relaxed, uninterrupted transitions between the partials of the trumpet.
Tip: Focus on the fact that you are simply playing one long steady stream of air. Imagining the sounds "tah" on lower notes and "ee" on upper notes may help move your air.

THU

Workout #284 **Type:** Interval **Sub-type:** Arpeggio
Goal: To hear each interval in your head, and then to execute it through the trumpet.
Tip: Try singing these exercises to ensure that your ears are truly hearing each note.

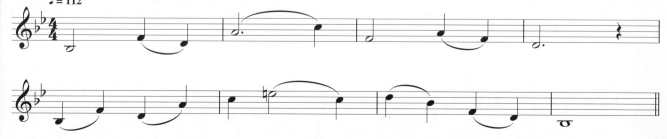

FRI

Workout #285 **Type:** Fingers **Sub-type:** Chromatic whole steps

Goal: To achieve agile, in-time, dexterous fingers.

Tip: Use a metronome and subdivide in your head. Every note should be perfectly in time.

SAT

Workout #286 **Type:** Variety **Sub-type:** Effects – falls

Goal: To fall off of a note in the jazz/commercial style.

Tip: There are a few different ways to play falls. For this example, transition from the valved note to a half valve as you are dropping off of the note. The result is a smoother fall.

SUN

Workout #287 **Type:** Etude **Sub-type:** C Lydian

Goal: To play musically and beautifully by utilizing the skills developed over the course of the week.

Tip: Internalize the sound of the F#s. This note, scale degree 4, is the most colorful note of the Lydian mode.

MON

Workout #288   **Type:** Scale   **Sub-type:** C Phrygian

Goals: 1) To develop an even, beautiful sound across the full range of the trumpet; 2) To reach the point in which you are no longer consciously thinking about the fingerings.

Note: A Phrygian scale can be thought of as a natural minor scale with an additional lowered scale degree 2.

TUE

Workout #289   **Type:** Articulation   **Sub-type:** Legato, staccato

Goal: To incorporate contrasting styles of articulation together.

Tip: Although the articulations are contrasting, strive to connect them to form one musical phrase.

WED

Workout #290   **Type:** Flexibility

Goal: To play relaxed, uninterrupted transitions between the partials of the trumpet.

Tip: Focus on the fact that you are simply playing one long steady stream of air. Imagining the sounds "tah" on lower notes and "ee" on upper notes may help move your air.

THU

Workout #291   **Type:** Interval   **Sub-type:** Expanding

Goal: To hear each interval in your head, and then to execute it through the trumpet.

Tip: Try singing these exercises to ensure that your ears are truly hearing each note. Imagine the wider intervals as being close together and easy to execute.

Workout #292 **Type:** Fingers **Sub-type:** Chromatic whole steps

Goal: To achieve agile, in-time, dexterous fingers.

Tip: Use a metronome and subdivide in your head. Every note should be perfectly in time.

FRI

Workout #293 **Type:** Variety **Sub-type:** Effects – shakes

Goal: To execute a jazz/commercial-style shake.

Tip: Aim your air at the upper partial and gently shake the trumpet with your right hand. Listen to the big bands listed on page 4 use this technique and copy the sound you hear.

SAT

Workout #294 **Type:** Etude **Sub-type:** C Phrygian

Goal: To play musically and beautifully by utilizing the skills developed over the course of the week.

Tip: Be extremely free with the time. Play this similarly to how someone would speak or chant, speeding up and slowing down naturally.

SUN

WEEK 43

MON

Workout #295   **Type:** Scale   **Sub-type:** C Locrian

Goals: 1) To develop an even, beautiful sound across the full range of the trumpet; 2) To reach the point in which you are no longer consciously thinking about the fingerings.

Note: A Locrian scale can be thought of as a natural minor scale with an additional lowered scale degrees 2 and 5.

TUE

Workout #296   **Type:** Articulation   **Sub-type:** Marcato, accent

Goal: To play both types of front-heavy articulations with strength.

Tip: Keep the marcatos pointed, but make sure they still have a full body of sound.

WED

Workout #297   **Type:** Flexibility

Goal: To play relaxed, uninterrupted transitions between the partials of the trumpet.

Tip: Focus on the fact that you are simply playing one long steady stream of air. Imagining the sounds "tah" on lower notes and "ee" on upper notes may help move your air.

THU

Workout #298   **Type:** Interval   **Sub-type:** Pattern

Goal: To hear each interval in your head, and then to execute it through the trumpet.

Tip: Try singing these exercises to ensure that your ears are truly hearing each note.

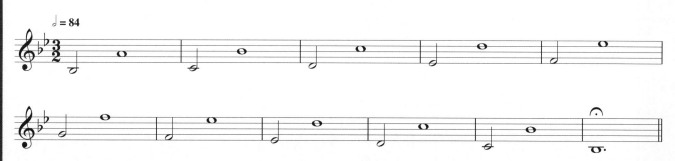

FRI

Workout #299　　　　　　　　**Type:** Fingers　　　　　　　　**Sub-type:** Chromatic threes

Goal: To achieve agile, in-time, dexterous fingers.
Tip: Use a metronome and subdivide in your head. Every note should be perfectly in time.

SAT

Workout #300　　　　　　　　**Type:** Variety　　　　　　　　**Sub-type:** Effects – portamento

Goal: To connect two notes musically with a quick chromatic run.
Tip: Practice slowly and deliberately at first. The end result should be a quick gesture. Have fun and be a little cheesy with it.

SUN

Workout #301　　　　　　　　**Type:** Etude　　　　　　　　**Sub-type:** C Locrian

Goal: To play musically and beautifully by utilizing the skills developed over the course of the week.
Tip: Passages like measure 5 are the reason we practice scales.

MON

Workout #302   **Type:** Scale   **Sub-type:** C Lydian Dominant

Goals: 1) To develop an even, beautiful sound across the full range of the trumpet; 2) To reach the point in which you are no longer consciously thinking about the fingerings.

Note: A Lydian Dominant scale can be thought of as a Mixolydian scale with a raised scale degree 4.

TUE

Workout #303   **Type:** Articulation   **Sub-type:** Double tongue

Goal: To produce a fast, clean, and even double tongue.

Tip: First practice by actually saying "ka" out loud, and then alternating between "ta" and "ka." Feel where your tongue hits the roof of your mouth. Replicate this feeling while playing the trumpet.

WED

Workout #304   **Type:** Flexibility

Goal: To play relaxed, uninterrupted transitions between the partials of the trumpet.

Tip: Focus on the fact that you are simply playing one long steady stream of air. Imagining the sounds "tah" on lower notes and "ee" on upper notes may help move your air.

THU

Workout #305   **Type:** Interval   **Sub-type:** Arpeggio

Goal: To hear each interval in your head, and then to execute it through the trumpet.

Tip: Try singing these exercises to ensure that your ears are truly hearing each note.

FRI

Workout #306

Type: Fingers **Sub-type:** Chromatic threes

Goal: To achieve agile, in-time, dexterous fingers.

Tip: Use a metronome and subdivide in your head. Every note should be perfectly in time.

SAT

Workout #307

Type: Variety **Sub-type:** Effects – portamento

Goal: To connect two notes musically with a quick scalar run.

Tip: Practice slowly and deliberately at first. The end result should be a quick gesture. Have fun and be a little cheesy with it.

SUN

Workout #308

Type: Etude **Sub-type:** C Lydian Dominant

Goal: To play musically and beautifully by utilizing the skills developed over the course of the week.

Tip: Internalize the sound of the F♯s and B♭s together. This is a sound uniquely characteristic to the Lydian Dominant scale.

MON

Workout #309   **Type:** Scale   **Sub-type:** C, Eb, F#, A diminished

Goals: 1) To develop an even, beautiful sound across the full range of the trumpet; 2) To reach the point in which you are no longer consciously thinking about the fingerings.

Note: The diminished scale is also symmetrical. Because of this, the scales listed in the Sub-type all share the same notes.

TUE

Workout #310   **Type:** Articulation   **Sub-type:** Double tongue

Goal: To produce a fast, clean, and even double tongue.

Tip: First practice by actually saying "ka" out loud, and then alternating between "ta" and "ka." Feel where your tongue hits the roof of your mouth. Replicate this feeling while playing the trumpet.

WED

Workout #311   **Type:** Flexibility

Goal: To play relaxed, uninterrupted transitions between the partials of the trumpet.

Tip: Focus on the fact that you are simply playing one long steady stream of air. Imagining the sounds "tah" on lower notes and "ee" on upper notes may help move your air.

THU

Workout #312   **Type:** Interval   **Sub-type:** Expanding

Goal: To hear each interval in your head, and then to execute it through the trumpet.

Tip: Try singing these exercises to ensure that your ears are truly hearing each note. Imagine the wider intervals as being close together and easy to execute.

FRI

Workout #313   **Type:** Fingers   **Sub-type:** Chromatic threes

Goal: To achieve agile, in-time, dexterous fingers.

Tip: Use a metronome and subdivide in your head. Every note should be perfectly in time.

SAT

Workout #314   **Type:** Variety   **Sub-type:** Effects – scoops

Goal: To execute a jazz/commercial style scoop into a note.

Tip: There are a few different ways to accomplish the scoop: 1) Lip bend into the note; 2) Half valve into the note; 3) Ease in your first or third valve slide as you begin the note (only if the note uses the valve you are sliding).

SUN

Workout #315   **Type:** Etude   **Sub-type:** C diminished

Goal: To play musically and beautifully by utilizing the skills developed over the course of the week.

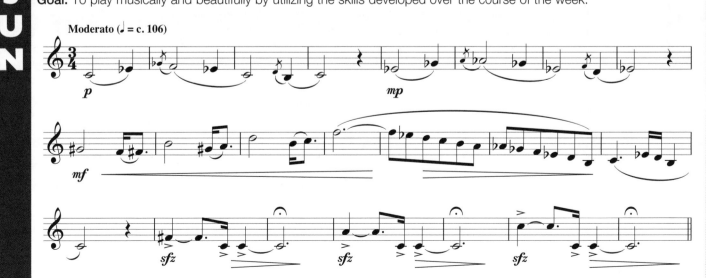

WEEK 46

MON

Workout #316   **Type:** Scale   **Sub-type:** C#, E, G, B♭ diminished

Goals: 1) To develop an even, beautiful sound across the full range of the trumpet; 2) To reach the point in which you are no longer consciously thinking about the fingerings.

Note: The diminished scale is also symmetrical. Because of this, the scales listed in the Sub-type share the same notes.

TUE

Workout #317   **Type:** Articulation   **Sub-type:** Double tongue

Goal: To produce a fast, clean, and even double tongue.

Tip: First practice by actually saying "ka" out loud, and then alternating between "ta" and "ka." Feel where your tongue hits the roof of your mouth. Replicate this feeling while playing the trumpet.

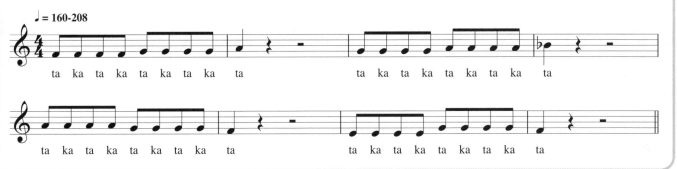

WED

Workout #318   **Type:** Flexibility

Goal: To play relaxed, uninterrupted transitions between the partials of the trumpet.

Tip: Focus on the fact that you are simply playing one long steady stream of air. Imagining the sounds "tah" on lower notes and "ee" on upper notes may help move your air.

THU

Workout #319   **Type:** Interval   **Sub-type:** Pattern

Goal: To hear each interval in your head, and then to execute it through the trumpet.

Tip: Try singing these exercises to ensure that your ears are truly hearing each note.

FRI

Workout #320 **Type:** Fingers **Sub-type:** Chromatic threes

Goal: To achieve agile, in-time, dexterous fingers.

Tip: Use a metronome and subdivide in your head. Every note should be perfectly in time.

SAT

Workout #321 **Type:** Variety **Sub-type:** Effects – tremolo

Goal: To play a rapid tremolo by using an alternate fingering.

Tip: Rapidly alternate between the normal fingering and the alternate fingering to create this harsh-sounding effect. Adjust your first or third valve slides so that the two fingerings are in tune with each other.

SUN

Workout #322 **Type:** Etude **Sub-type:** G diminished

Goal: To play musically and beautifully by utilizing the skills developed over the course of the week.

Tip: Be over-the-top with this one. Exaggerate accents and crescendos, and as always, have fun with it.

MON

Workout #323

Type: Scale

Sub-type: D, F, A♭, B diminished

Goals: 1) To develop an even, beautiful sound across the full range of the trumpet; 2) To reach the point in which you are no longer consciously thinking about the fingerings.

Note: The diminished scale is also symmetrical. Because of this, the scales listed in the Sub-type share the same notes.

TUE

Workout #324

Type: Articulation

Sub-type: Triple tongue

Goal: To produce a fast, clean, and even triple tongue.

Tip: First practice by saying "ta ta ka" out loud, feeling where your tongue hits the roof of your mouth. Then say multiple "ta ta kas" in a row. Once this is more comfortable, replicate the feeling through the trumpet.

WED

Workout #325

Type: Flexibility

Goal: To play relaxed, uninterrupted transitions between the partials of the trumpet.

Tip: Focus on the fact that you are simply playing one long steady stream of air. Imagining the sounds "tah" on lower notes and "ee" on upper notes may help move your air.

THU

Workout #326

Type: Interval

Sub-type: Arpeggio

Goal: To hear each interval in your head, and then to execute it through the trumpet.

Tip: Try singing these exercises to ensure that your ears are truly hearing each note.

Workout #327   **Type:** Fingers   **Sub-type:** Chromatic threes
Goal: To achieve agile, in-time, dexterous fingers.
Tip: Use a metronome and subdivide in your head. Every note should be perfectly in time.

Workout #328   **Type:** Variety   **Sub-type:** Effects – glissando
Goal: To execute a smooth glissando by using the half valve.
Tip: Listen to the clarinet solo at the beginning of Gershwin's *Rhapsody in Blue*. That sound is exactly what you should be emulating.

Workout #329   **Type:** Etude   **Sub-type:** E diminished
Goal: To play musically and beautifully by utilizing the skills developed over the course of the week.
Tip: Give this one some Spanish flair.

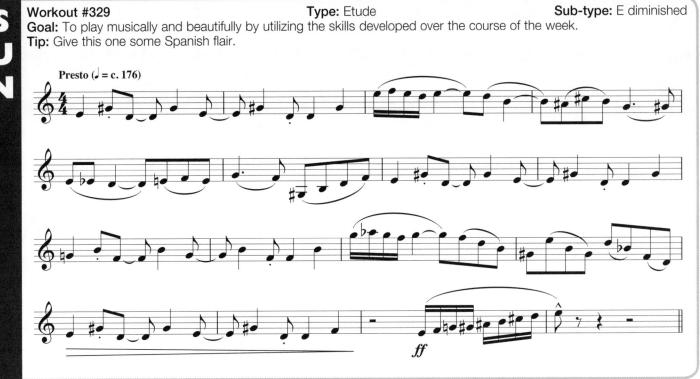

WEEK 48

MON

Workout #330　　　　**Type:** Scale　　　　**Sub-type:** C/E/A♭ Augmented, D/F♯/B♭ Augmented
Goals: 1) To develop an even, beautiful sound across the full range of the trumpet; 2) To reach the point in which you are no longer consciously thinking about the fingerings.
Note: The augmented scale is also symmetrical. Because of this, the scales listed in the Sub-type share the same notes.

♩ = 86-180

C augmented

D augmented

TUE

Workout #331　　　　**Type:** Articulation　　　　**Sub-type:** Triple tongue
Goal: To produce a fast, clean, and even triple tongue.
Tip: First practice by saying "ta ta ka" out loud, feeling where your tongue hits the roof of your mouth. Then say multiple "ta ta kas" in a row. Once this is more comfortable, replicate the feeling through the trumpet.

♩ = 144

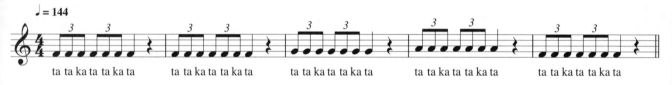

ta ta ka ta ta ka ta　　　ta ta ka ta ta ka ta　　　ta ta ka ta ta ka ta　　　ta ta ka ta ta ka ta　　　ta ta ka ta ta ka ta

WED

Workout #332　　　　**Type:** Flexibility
Goal: To play relaxed, uninterrupted transitions between the partials of the trumpet.
Tip: Focus on the fact that you are simply playing one long steady stream of air. Imagining the sounds "tah" on lower notes and "ee" on upper notes may help move your air.

♩ = 104

THU

Workout #333　　　　**Type:** Interval　　　　**Sub-type:** Expanding (augmented)
Goal: To hear each interval in your head, and then to execute it through the trumpet.
Tip: Try singing these exercises to ensure that your ears are truly hearing each note. Imagine the wider intervals as being close together and easy to execute.

♩ = 84

FRI

Workout #334 **Type:** Fingers **Sub-type:** Chromatic threes

Goal: To achieve agile, in-time, dexterous fingers.

Tip: Use a metronome and subdivide in your head. Every note should be perfectly in time.

SAT

Workout #335 **Type:** Variety **Sub-type:** Effects – doit/squeeze

Goal: To execute a jazz/commercial style doit.

Tip: Play the written note, then move the note upward in range as far as you'd like. Half-valving the squeeze results in the technique sounding more fluid.

SUN

Workout #336 **Type:** Etude **Sub-type:** D augmented

Goal: To play musically and beautifully by utilizing the skills developed over the course of the week.

Tip: Be very expressive. Take your time on the rest with a fermata. Silence is an important part of music.

MON

Workout #337 **Type:** Scale **Sub-type:** Db/F/A Augmented, Eb/G/B Augmented
Goals: 1) To develop an even, beautiful sound across the full range of the trumpet; 2) To reach the point in which you are no longer consciously thinking about the fingerings.
Note: The augmented scale is also symmetrical. Because of this, the scales listed in the Sub-type share the same notes.

TUE

Workout #338 **Type:** Articulation **Sub-type:** Triple tongue
Goal: To produce a fast, clean, and even triple tongue.
Tip: First practice by saying "ta ta kas" out loud, feeling where your tongue hits the roof of your mouth. Then say multiple "ta ta kas" in a row. Once this is more comfortable, replicate the feeling through the trumpet.

WED

Workout #339 **Type:** Flexibility
Goal: To play relaxed, uninterrupted transitions between the partials of the trumpet.
Tip: Use a metronome to make sure that each increase in speed is perfectly in time.

THU

Workout #340 **Type:** Interval **Sub-type:** Pattern
Goal: To hear each interval in your head, and then to execute it through the trumpet.
Tip: Try singing these exercises to ensure that your ears are truly hearing each note.

FRI

Workout #341   **Type:** Fingers   **Sub-type:** Chromatic fours

Goal: To achieve agile, in-time, dexterous fingers.

Tip: Use a metronome and subdivide in your head. Every note should be perfectly in time.

SAT

Workout #342   **Type:** Variety   **Sub-type:** Effects – growl

Goal: To create a raspy, bluesy tone quality.

Tip: There are three ways of producing this effect: 1) Humming through the trumpet while playing; 2) Vibrating the back of the throat, almost like you are gargling or clearing your throat; 3) Flutter-tonguing: letting the tip of the tongue rapidly vibrate as if you were rolling an "R" in Spanish.

SUN

Workout #343   **Type:** Etude   **Sub-type:** G♯ minor mixed meter

Goal: To play musically and beautifully by utilizing the skills developed over the course of the week.

Tip: Feel and internalize the unique groove of the 7/4. Try counting the pulse as 1–2, 1–2, 1–2–3.

MON

Workout #344 **Type:** Scale **Sub-type:** C blues
Goals: 1) To develop an even, beautiful sound across the full range of the trumpet; 2) To reach the point in which you are no longer consciously thinking about the fingerings.
Tip: Try to emulate a blues vocalist and how they shape each note with this scale.

TUE

Workout #345 **Type:** Articulation **Sub-type:** Jazz – Swing eighths
(tongue one, slur two, slur two)

Goal: To execute this swing/bebop style of articulating.
Tip: Practice slowly at first to avoid becoming tongue-tied. This pattern of articulating will begin to feel natural after repetition.

WED

Workout #346 **Type:** Flexibility
Goal: To play relaxed, uninterrupted transitions between the partials of the trumpet.
Tip: Use a metronome to make sure that each increase in speed is perfectly in time.

THU

Workout #347 **Type:** Interval
Goal: To hear each interval in your head, and then to execute it through the trumpet.
Tip: Try singing these exercises to ensure that your ears are truly hearing each note.

Workout #348 **Type:** Fingers **Sub-type:** Chromatic fours

Goal: To achieve agile, in-time, dexterous fingers.

Tip: Use a metronome and subdivide in your head. Every note should be perfectly in time.

Workout #349 **Type:** Variety **Sub-type:** Upper register

Goal: To produce high notes that sound effortless without too much lip pressure or muscle strain.

Tip: Your focus should be on moving a fast, condensed stream of air. The notes may come out quietly at first. Volume will come as your embouchure gains muscle.

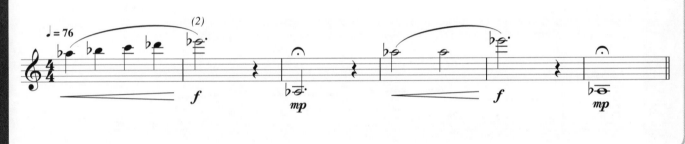

Workout #350 **Type:** Etude **Sub-type:** C blues

Goal: To play musically and beautifully by utilizing the skills developed over the course of the week.

Tip: Feel the groove, imagine a drum set playing behind you.

MON

Workout #351
Type: Scale   **Sub-type:** C major pentatonic, A minor pentatonic
Goals: 1) To develop an even, beautiful sound across the full range of the trumpet; 2) To reach the point in which you are no longer consciously thinking about the fingerings.
Tip: This set of two scales uses the same notes, but they sound different depending on which note is emphasized.

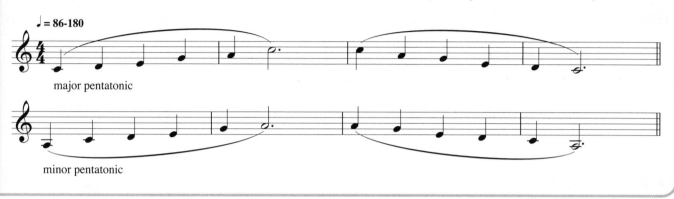

TUE

Workout #352
Type: Articulation   **Sub-type:** Jazz – ghost notes
Goal: To ghost certain notes of the musical line in a jazz-like fashion.
Tip: Play the parenthesized notes significantly softer than the surrounding notes.

WED

Workout #353
Type: Flexibility
Goal: To play relaxed, uninterrupted transitions between the partials of the trumpet.
Tip: Use a metronome to make sure that each increase in speed is perfectly in time.

THU

Workout #354
Type: Interval   **Sub-type:** Expanding
Goal: To hear each interval in your head, and then to execute it through the trumpet.
Tip: Try singing these exercises to ensure that your ears are truly hearing each note. Imagine the wider intervals as being close together and easy to execute.

Workout #355　　　　　　　**Type:** Fingers　　　　　　**Sub-type:** Chromatic fours

Goal: To achieve agile, in-time, dexterous fingers.

Tip: Use a metronome and subdivide in your head. Every note should be perfectly in time.

Workout #356　　　　　　　**Type:** Variety　　　　　　**Sub-type:** Upper register

Goal: To produce high notes that sound effortless without too much lip pressure or muscle strain.

Tip: Your focus should be on moving a fast, condensed stream of air. The notes may come out quietly at first. Volume will come as your embouchure gains muscle.

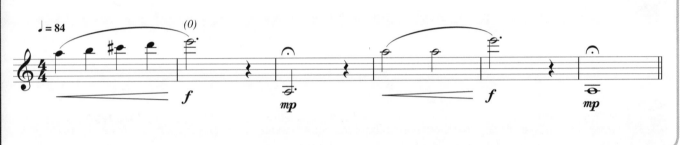

Workout #357　　　　　　　**Type:** Etude　　　　　　**Sub-type:** A minor pentatonic mixed meter

Goal: To play musically and beautifully by utilizing the skills developed over the course of the week.

Tip: Feel the groove created by the 5/4 meter. This example is counted 1–2–3, 1–2. Listen to "Take 5" by Dave Brubeck.

MON

Workout #358 **Type:** Scale **Sub-type:** C dominant bebop, C major bebop
Goals: 1) To develop an even, beautiful sound across the full range of the trumpet; 2) To reach the point in which you are no longer consciously thinking about the fingerings.
Tip: The dominant bebop scale is similar to the Mixolydian scale, except it includes an additional half step between 1 and 7. The major bebop scale is the same as the major scale, with an additional half step between 6 and 5. This organizes the scales in such way that the important notes end up on the strong beats of the measure.

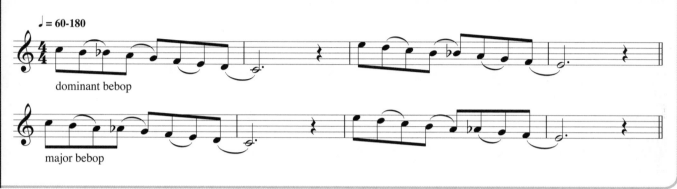

TUE

Workout #359 **Type:** Articulation **Sub-type:** Jazz – offbeat weight
Goal: To stress and add weight to every offbeat in a jazz fashion.
Tip: This style of emphasizing offbeats is common in Big Band writing.

WED

Workout #360 **Type:** Flexibility **Sub-type:** Lip trill
Goal: To produce an even, relaxed, rapid alteration between the partials of the trumpet.
Tip: Alternating quickly between "tah" and "ee" may help to produce the effect. Always keep your air moving.

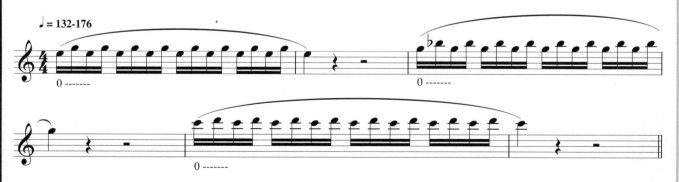

THU

Workout #361 **Type:** Interval **Sub-type:** Pattern

Goal: To hear each interval in your head, and then to execute it through the trumpet.
Tip: Try singing these exercises to ensure that your ears are truly hearing each note.

FRI

Workout #362 **Type:** Fingers **Sub-type:** Chromatic fours

Goal: To achieve agile, in-time, dexterous fingers.
Tip: Use a metronome and subdivide in your head. Every note should be perfectly in time.

SAT

Workout #363 **Type:** Variety **Sub-type:** Upper register

Goal: To produce high notes that sound effortless without too much lip pressure or muscle strain.
Tip: Your focus should be on moving a fast, condensed stream of air. The notes may come out quietly at first. Volume will come as your embouchure gains muscle.

SUN

Workout #364 **Type:** Etude **Sub-type:** C bebop

Goal: To play musically and beautifully by utilizing the skills developed over the course of the week.
Tip: This etude incorporates the C dominant bebop scale, F major bebop scale, and E♭ dominant bebop scales. Knowing your scales beforehand makes passages like these seem easy.

DAY 365

Workout #365   **Type:** Duet

Goal: This duet is for two trumpets in B♭. Find a friend and make some music together!

Tip: Always blend your sound with the musicians you play with. When the melody alternates between voices, for example in measures 3 and 4, the resulting line should sound seamless. Be a team working together in perfect harmony.

INDEX

ACKNOWLEDGMENTS

I would like to extend my sincerest gratitude to everyone who made this book possible:

- Dave Baker, my lifelong partner-in-crime, for the years of bouncing trumpet ideas off of each other and for the vital writing assistance.

- Jeff Schroedl at Hal Leonard for presenting me with the incredible opportunity of writing this book, as well as J. Mark Baker at Hal Leonard for assembling all of the material together in such a precise and aesthetic manner.

- All of the trumpet instructors and music educators who have guided me since the very beginning, including John Rommel, Joey Tartell, Pat Harbison, Jack Sutte, John Brndiar, Alex Jokipii, Kevin Duncan, Christine Riederer, Ben Albright, and Ivan Albright.

- The brass colleagues that I am lucky to call my friends, Dan Egan, Andy Lott, Joe Anderson, Grant Smiley, Sam Wells, Cean Robinson, and Jon Morawski, for collaborating on our list of favorite brass recordings.

- My dear friends Rory O'Connor, Melinda Ho, Jess Henry, Jordan Lawson, Alicia Salgato, Haley Sorensen, and Carol Castiglione, for acting as a second pair of eyes and a source of constant encouragement.

- Dan Figureli at Primary Sound Studios for the expertise in recording the audio tracks.

Finally, I extend my deepest thanks to my parents, Thomas and Linda Johnson, for their endless support of my musical endeavors.

ABOUT THE AUTHOR

A versatile, genre-crossing freelance musician, **Kevin Johnson** performs throughout the United States. He has appeared with a variety of ensembles ranging from the Columbus, Owensboro, and Carmel Symphony Orchestras, to jazz and Latin ensembles such as Cleveland's Mojo Big Band and Sammy de Leon y Su Orquesta. Johnson has shared the stage with Broadway sensation Ciara Renée at 54 Below in New York City, performed with the Cleveland Orchestra's Blossom Festival Band, and accompanied the New York Voices with the Brent Wallarab Jazz Ensemble at Jazz at Lincoln Center. In addition to trumpet, Johnson is heard regularly on guitar and keyboards with various musical theater companies. Most recently, Johnson joined Carnival Cruise Line's *Splendor* as a member of the show band.

Ben Meadors Photography

In addition to his life as a performer, Johnson has a passion for directing, arranging, and composing music. Working side by side with Steve Zegree, Johnson held the position of bandleader and arranger for the Singing Hoosiers. He has served as assistant director of vocal music at Charles F. Brush High School, and assistant director of the Roberto Ocasio Latin Jazz Camp. His love of the Beatles led him to co-found the BWBeatles, acting as music director of the *Abbey Road, Sgt. Pepper's Lonely Hearts Club Band*, and *Magical Mystery Tour concerts*. Johnson's composition "Donut" was featured at Bloomington's Jazz Celebration featuring John Fedchock. His solo trumpet piece "The Seventh Trumpet" was released on Jack Sutte's album, *Fanfare Alone*.

A native of Niagara Falls, New York, Johnson attended the Baldwin Wallace Conservatory of Music where he studied with Jack Sutte of The Cleveland Orchestra, graduating magna cum laude with a Bachelor of Music degree in Trumpet Performance. He subsequently earned a Master of Music degree in Jazz Studies from the Jacobs School of Music at Indiana University, studying with John Rommel and Pat Harbison.

Johnson's previous publications for Hal Leonard Corporation include *The Beatles Session Parts*, a collection of 20 note-for-note scored transcriptions of the Beatles' session players' string, woodwind, and brass parts